# TRAVEL FITNESS

**Rebecca Johnson**
**Bill Tulin, CSCS**

**Human Kinetics**

)ging-in-Publication Data

lin.

p.    cm.
Includes bibliographical references and index.
ISBN 0-87322-655-0 (pbk.)
1. Travel--Health aspects.  I. Tulin, Bill, 1958-    .  II.  Title.
RA783.5.J54     1995
613.6'8--dc20                                              95-1294
                                                          CIP

ISBN: 0-87322-655-0

**Developmental Editor:** Rodd Whelpley; **Assistant Editors:** Jacqueline Blakley and Kent Reel; **Copyeditor:** Karen Bankston; **Proofreader:** Amy Wilson; **Indexer:** Theresa Schaefer; **Typesetter:** Sandra Meier; **Text Designer:** Jody Boles; **Layout Artist:** Tara Welsch; **Cover Designer:** Keith Blomberg; **Photographer (cover):** Wilmer Zehr; **Illustrator:** Susan Carson; **Printer:** United Graphics

Human Kinetics books are available at special discounts for bulk purchase. Special editions or book excerpts can also be created to specification. For details, contact the Special Sales Manager at Human Kinetics.

Printed in the United States of America

10  9  8  7  6  5  4  3  2

**Human Kinetics**
Web site: http://www.humankinetics.com/

*United States:* Human Kinetics, P.O. Box 5076, Champaign, IL 61825-5076
1-800-747-4457
e-mail: humank@hkusa.com

*Canada:* Human Kinetics, Box 24040, Windsor, ON N8Y 4Y9
1-800-465-7301 (in Canada only)
e-mail: humank@hkcanada.com

*Europe:* Human Kinetics, P.O. Box IW14, Leeds LS16 6TR, United Kingdom
(44) 1132 781708
e-mail: humank@hkeurope.com

*Australia:* Human Kinetics, 57A Price Avenue, Lower Mitcham, South Australia 5062
(08) 277 1555
e-mail: humank@hkaustralia.com

*New Zealand:* Human Kinetics, P.O. Box 105-231, Auckland 1
(09) 523 3462
e-mail: humank@hknewz.com

To all those who have experienced the challenge
of staying fit on the road and want to meet it

# *Contents*

# *Foreword*

This is a wonderful book!

Very rarely can authors workably blend two enormous and disparate disciplines into a coherent whole and make it entertaining. Rebecca Johnson and Bill Tulin have done just that. They have combined sound advice on fitness with extensive and interesting information available only to seasoned travelers. Bravo!

When the authors interviewed me for this ambitious project, I had to applaud their courage but, at the same time, question their sanity. Writing a good book on fitness is difficult enough without the added challenge of saying anything meaningful to the frequent traveler about how to manage "fitness on the road." But Rebecca and Bill accomplish this task with flair and creativity. They've talked to all the right experts (both fitness professionals and fitness-conscious travelers), and they paid their dues both in the gym and at the ticket counter.

As a fitness researcher and frequent traveler (I log over 200,000 miles a year on speaking engagements and consulting), I approach this topic with both personal and professional passion. I am also a critical consumer of this type of information. So with great pleasure I notice that the authors have picked up on many of the subtle details of remaining fit on the road. They handle the basics extremely well—from hydration to preparation to jet lag. But they also delve into subtleties only known to serous travelers. Do you know why it is important not to have your wallet in your back pocket on a trans-Atlantic flight? You will. (And I thought it was just *my* secret.)

Fitness during travel is an important topic. All too often I have seen well-intentioned executives abandon their fitness routines because of travel. I *never* leave home without my fitness equipment (it is even more important than my American Express card). *Travel Fitness* is a gem of a book and is must reading for every traveler and every fitness professional who advises them.

James M. Rippe, M.D.

# Preface

If you're like most harried travelers, you just don't feel like yourself on the road. How could you? You're catapulted from your comfortable home and work environments, shuttled across time zones, often subjected to the indignities of air travel, and pressured to perform in an unfamiliar setting under tight money and time constraints. Your spouse or children may resent your being on the road so often. And your travel schedule leaves you with little time to exercise, eat, or sleep right. These physical and mental stressors challenge the body's adaptive mechanism—and can leave you burned out. *Travel* is derived from the French word *travailler,* meaning to work, and that's exactly what our bodies and minds must do to maintain fitness and balance while enduring the physical and mental demands of travel.

We know—we've been there. Our work has taken us on the road more than we care to remember. Too often, our health suffered. That's why we wrote this book. We wanted to learn what could be done to feel better while traveling. Why is it that some travelers stay fit, while others gain weight, feel lousy, and barely cope? Why do some business travelers maintain their mental alertness, while others perform below par? What really separates the winners from the losers in the travel game? To find the answers to these and other questions, we interviewed hundreds of fit travelers, fitness experts, sleep doctors, nutritionists, psychologists, and research scientists. What we learned and what we share in *Travel Fitness* are the best ways for frequent travelers like you to meet the fitness challenge.

We found that the hardest tasks for virtually every traveler were maintaining the health and fitness routines established at home and the sheer challenge of staying fit in a new environment. Many also were overcome by the abundant temptations of the road. How often have rich food, alcohol, stress, lack of time, or inadequate fitness facilities sidetracked your fitness regimen?

Odds are, leaving home with the vague intention of "doing better this time" won't solve your travel fitness problems. Whatever your concerns, you need a specific plan for staying fit on the road. We've written this book to help you identify which of your travel habits need changing and to help you tackle each area of concern. All the raw materials you need—the expert advice, practical wisdom, and scientifically backed strategies—are here in the pages of *Travel Fitness*.

Here's some of what you'll learn:

- How to plan a complete health and fitness itinerary that works for you
- How to improve how you feel after a long flight or car ride
- The latest strategies for coping with jet lag
- Six principles for working out on the road
- How to enjoy restaurant meals without gaining weight
- The best ways to recognize and manage travel-induced stress
- How to enhance the quality of your sleep while traveling
- The best ways to handle separation from loved ones
- Strategies for achieving a fast recovery after a trip

We won't try to sell you on a particular approach to travel fitness—only you can decide what works for you. Total wellness and balance on the road depend on the simple act of building healthy practices into your travel plans. There aren't grand designs or quick fixes for feeling better on the road. Your success depends on the many small choices you make each day that you are away from home. Will you pass on dessert or indulge because you feel lonely? Will you visit the hotel fitness room or drink with colleagues in the bar? Will you walk to your meeting or take a cab? The successful travelers we interviewed all had discovered ingenious ways of staying fit on the road and avoiding away-from-home distractions. They weren't just surviving the road, they were thriving. For them, travel was more than an annoyance to be endured en route to achieving career success—they actually *enjoyed* it.

Whether you're a traveling executive or salesperson who loses your edge on the road, an athlete who must compete away from home, or a vacationer with a full itinerary, you, too, can bridge the gap between how you feel at home and while traveling. You, too, can learn to achieve "travel fitness," a state of physical, mental, and emotional balance that allows you to feel and act like a winner.

We invite you to take on the challenge and to build fitness and vitality into your travel plans. Start by incorporating one or more of the tips in this book on your next trip. You don't have to change everything at once. Even small changes can produce immediate fitness benefits. As you read through *Travel Fitness*, focus on the chapters that address your top fitness concerns. You may even want to read those chapters first. Note the tips, strategies, and options that seem most helpful to you. Over time, you'll develop a travel fitness program that works. The payoff in physical well-being, mental alertness, and better job performance will make it well worth your efforts.

Travel may involve hard work, but it doesn't have to torment your body or suppress your spirit. You *can* win the travel fitness game, and feel better on your next trip and on all the trips that follow.

# *Acknowledgments*

Sincere thanks and appreciation to the following individuals who made this book possible:

- The many people who shared their stories of life on the road
- The research scientists, medical doctors, fitness experts, nutritionists, psychologists, and other experts for their insight and advice on achieving travel fitness
- Katherine M. Johnson, for her generous support, research, and imaginative problem solving
- Mary McLoughlin, for always being there
- Susan McFadden, for her hard work and great ideas
- Our families, for their love and encouragement

# Planning Your Health and Fitness Itinerary

**T**ravel has a way of foiling the best fitness intentions. Tight scheduling, unfamiliar surroundings, and fatigue from jet lag make it too easy to lose our fitness regimens. Maybe you lament: "I just don't have the time or energy to concern myself with staying fit on the road." Besides, you may be wondering, Do I really need to worry about my fitness while traveling? Our answer: a resounding *yes*. With frequent travel, you run the risk of losing the benefits of your healthier practices at home—and feeling lousy while away. The mileage takes too much of a toll if you eat fat-laden foods and remain sedentary most of the trip. "When you're on the road, you're under more stress than at most other times. Your fitness program becomes more important, not less," says Dr. James Rippe, director of the exercise physiology and nutrition laboratory at the University of Massachusetts Medical School. To perform at your peak, free of the many nagging bodily complaints induced by travel, you need to preserve at least a semblance of your fitness routine.

But how? Getting a handle on your travel fitness requires one thing above all else: the commitment to do it. Too many of us focus on business or sightseeing goals, to the exclusion of our fitness goals. We may have mastered the intricacies of frequent flier programs, but we haven't a clue how to find a safe place to jog at our destination.

Either you're going to control travel, or travel is going to control you. You decide. It's not impossible, or even that difficult, to pay attention to fitness while on the road. Even small changes, squeezed in during a few free minutes here and there, can make a difference in how you feel.

To change your travel habits, planning ahead is key, and it doesn't take a monumental effort. "It's just a matter of being somewhat conscious that having a fitness program on the road is critical and doing a little extra planning. Most people falter because they don't plan ahead at all," says Rippe.

We're not advocating that you become an uptight slave to your body, fastidiously monitoring your diet and exercise routines while on the road. We want you to have a good time—we just think that planning for and adhering to a sensible fitness routine while away will help you do that.

In this chapter, we'll get you started designing your own travel fitness program, offer you tips on how to pack smart, and give you the lowdown on international fitness planning. But first, let's find out how you're currently managing your health and fitness while traveling. Take the following **Travel Fitness Audit** to find out.

## Travel Fitness Audit

Below are the seven major fitness areas affecting most travelers, all of which are addressed in *Travel Fitness*. Under each category are statements which may describe how you feel during or after a trip. Think back over your most recent trips. Place a check mark next to each statement that applies to you. Then, tally your responses. If you have one or more checks in a given category, place this on your list of travel fitness areas needing improvement. Use this information for goal setting. Pay special attention to the chapters covering the fitness topics of concern to you.

## 1. Fitness in Transit

❏ I often feel headachy or lightheaded after a flight.

❏ My body is stiff and achy when I get off the plane or after a drive.

❏ Occasionally, I'm nauseated during or after a flight or while driving.

❏ After most flights or drives, I'm very tired.

❏ I'm sometimes short of breath while flying.

❏ My neck and back hurt sometimes after a flight.

❏ I sometimes have ear discomfort, even pain, while in the air.

❏ During or after a flight, I'm often thirsty.

❏ I feel very anxious about flying.

## 2. Jet Lag

❏ I'm sometimes confused and disoriented after a long flight.

❏ My appetite isn't the same in a new time zone.

❏ I often can't get to sleep or wake up early in a new city.

❏ Sometimes I'll become extremely tired at odd times after crossing time zones.

❏ I'm often constipated after transmeridian travel.

❏ Even after I sleep, I don't feel rested.

❏ I find it difficult to concentrate or pay attention after flying.

❏ My memory isn't the same for the first few days after arriving.

❏ I sometimes feel clumsy or uncoordinated after flying.

## 3. Sleep

❏ I can't stay asleep even when I quickly fall to sleep on the road.

❏ I have a hard time winding down after a tough day of travel.

❏ It takes me more than 20 minutes to fall asleep in a new place.

❏ I often have coffee after dinner.

❏ Sometimes waves of fatigue come over me when I'm traveling.

❏ I rarely can wake up without an alarm clock.

❏ After a trip, I need more sleep.

❏ I often stay up late before a trip packing and getting ready.

❏ Occasionally I'll have a nightcap to help me get to sleep while away.

## 4. Exercise

❏ I'm often too busy or too tired to work out while traveling.

❏ I feel less flexible and limber after a trip.

❏ My pace is slower when I exercise on the road.

❏ After a trip, I notice that I'm not as strong as I was before I left.

❏ While traveling, I sometimes go three days or more without exercising.

❏ If I can't replicate my at-home workout, I don't bother exercising on the road.

❏ I've had some "close calls" with safety while working out in unfamiliar cities.

❏ When I travel I sometimes run out of options for keeping active.

❏ I don't feel comfortable working out in a new health club.

## 5. Diet

❏ Since I started traveling, I've gained weight.

❏ On the road, I feel very tired in the afternoon.

❏ My blood pressure and/or cholesterol are up since traveling.

❏ I have more attacks of heartburn and indigestion while traveling.

❏ I often "let loose" with my diet on the road.

❏ I rarely plan ahead by setting diet priorities before leaving.

❏ I'm frequently constipated on the road.

❏ When abroad, I'll try any new food once.

❏ While traveling, sometimes I eat just for something to do.

## 6. Stress

❏ I sometimes overreact to trivial irritations on the road.

❏ While traveling, I don't sleep well.

❏ I occasionally get palpitations when I travel.

❏ My thoughts sometimes race, and I can't pay attention at meetings.

❏ I get frustrated and angry when things don't go my way on a trip.

❏ I have more neck aches and back pain during or just after a trip.

❏ Before going to sleep, I double-check the locks on the doors and windows.

❏ I get more headaches on the road.

❏ I sometimes feel lightheaded, sweaty, or dizzy while traveling.

### 7. Separation

❏ I often miss birthdays, holidays, and other significant events because of travel.

❏ After a trip I sometimes feel distant from my family and friends.

❏ My partner feels resentful because I travel.

❏ I sometimes feel shut out of family life because I'm gone so much.

❏ Coming home, I'm so busy catching up that I sometimes don't schedule family time.

❏ Sometimes I'll schedule a trip because things are "getting to me" at home.

❏ My partner and I argue more frequently when I return.

❏ I feel guilty leaving my family at home.

❏ I have a hard time maintaining relationships because I'm not home enough.

# Designing Your Personal Travel Fitness Program

What did the Travel Fitness Audit reveal about your health and fitness on the road? What travel fitness areas are most challenging to you? Maybe you can't resist those rich desserts at business dinners and have gained a few pounds since traveling. Or too often you find yourself tossing and turning in a new bed, feeling dull and groggy the next day. Then diet and sleep are fitness concerns for you.

Using the results from the audit as a guide, take a few minutes to write in your specific **Travel Fitness Problem Areas** on the form provided (p. 6). How many check marks did each area receive in the audit? Place this number under "Score."

## *Travel Fitness Problem Areas*

| Travel fitness area | Score from fitness audit | Rank |
|---|---|---|
| Fitness in transit | _____ | _____ |
| Jet lag | _____ | _____ |
| Sleep | _____ | _____ |
| Exercise | _____ | _____ |
| Diet | _____ | _____ |
| Stress | _____ | _____ |
| Separation | _____ | _____ |

Now, think about the importance of each listed travel fitness area to you. A high score in a given area may flag a priority for you. If, for example, most of your check marks were under "stress," this is an obvious category to focus on. It may be that you scored higher for "jet lag" than "diet," even though keeping trim is of primary concern to you. In this case improving your diet would be a higher ranking goal than tackling jet lag. After you've assessed the relative importance of each fitness area, rank-order them from top to bottom, giving a rank of #1 to the area of greatest concern to you and continue down the list until you give the highest number to the area of least concern.

You've just accomplished the most difficult task in planning your personal travel health and fitness program—mapping your long-range goals. By identifying and setting priorities for the fitness areas you want to improve, you've created a clear and focused framework on which to build the rest of your plan. Keep a written list of your top goals in a place where you will see it, especially when you're on the road. If you travel with a pocket planner, write your goals in the planner and review them before and during each trip. Or tack a list of your goals inside your briefcase. The idea is to constantly remind yourself of what you want to achieve.

You know where you're headed. Now how will you get there? The key is to translate your long-range travel fitness objectives into shorter-term task or "to-do" lists. As you read through the pages of *Travel Fitness*, write down practical tips that will help you meet your long-range goals. These tips can become part of your task list. For example, if dining out is your fatal travel fitness flaw, you may decide to eat one meal a day in your hotel room to better control your caloric intake. How can you accomplish this? What specific actions will help you meet your goal? One item on your list might be packing healthy snacks that travel well, a tip mentioned in Chapter 6. Don't be afraid to give yourself a deadline for accomplishing items on your to-do list. Sometimes the best motivation is having to answer to yourself for a missed deadline.

Having a long-range plan translated into specific tasks means you're ready to take ACTION. The ultimate goal is to achieve travel fitness— total physical, mental, and emotional balance while on the road. But even a thousand-mile journey begins with the first step. While planning your fitness itinerary, remember that practicing just one new healthy habit on your next trip will put you on the road to feeling better.

## Pack With Fitness in Mind

There are as many philosophies of packing as there are travelers. Some folks want to be prepared for anything, cramming several bags for the chance encounter or freak weather occurrence. Others sacrifice the psychological security of toting along half their worldly possessions, opting for lightweight carry-ons. Few travelers, however, pack with fitness in mind. We urge you to rethink the way you pack. Make it your goal to pack in a way that accommodates your travel health and fitness commitments. Observe three basic principles of packing fit:

1. Focus on traveling light, especially when traveling by plane.

2. Make comfort a priority.

3. Pack to meet your specific health and fitness goals.

Avoiding what one travel writer dubbed "baggage-intensive travel" has two fitness benefits: bypassing the stress of checking bags and, possibly even more important, saving your back, neck, and shoulders the agony of transporting heavy luggage. Unless you're of the rare breed that views unwieldy bags as traveling fitness equipment (Think of all those calories burned lugging colossal suitcases through the terminal!), find a way to pare down your portables and opt for lightweight carry-on luggage. Among the veteran travelers we interviewed, one central packing axiom held sway: The more you travel, the less you carry. "My goal is to keep my baggage as light as possible," says Ellen Hollander, 36, who travels more than 200 days of the year as a regional manager for the Electric Power Research Institute in Washington, DC. "If you want to stay fit and healthy, you have to minimize what you carry because it can really hurt your neck and back. If you get off the plane and you're sore from carrying luggage, you won't want to work out that night," she says.

But how can you pare down what you carry? One common practice of savvy travelers: set out what you think you'll need and then put half of it back in the closet. Of course there's more leeway if you're traveling by car, but always try to travel light. As one traveler queried, "Unless the trip is social—will involve seeing the same people on more than several occasions, at a number of different events—why take more than a minimal wardrobe?" Really cull through what you're thinking of taking along. Is each item absolutely necessary? Visualize what you'll be doing on the trip and ask yourself, What's the minimum amount of clothing that I can get away with?

To cut back on clothes, pack around one color scheme—no shirts or blouses that match only one item. You get more mileage from clothes that you can mix and match. That way, it's easier to match accessories and shoes and you'll save on space. Think also about using clothes in more than one role. For example, a suit jacket can accompany a matching skirt or pants during the day and jeans at night. Watch the number of shoes you stuff into your suitcase—they're the heaviest things most of us pack. Wear your athletic shoes on the plane. You'll be ready to do some fitness walking in the airport, and you'll keep one of the chunkiest items out of your bags. Take advantage of travel sizes of shampoo, lotion, toothpaste, deodorant—they're great space savers. Call ahead to find out what services the hotel offers. If reasonably priced same-day cleaning service is available, why pack more than two suits or three or four shirts? Similarly, if you can obtain a blow dryer, iron, or other items from the hotel, you don't need to take them along. Says Hollander: "I've cut what I carry by 20 percent just by staying in a full service hotel."

Whatever you do, don't forget to consider how much your bags weigh empty. Quite often too much weight comes from the bags themselves. Ideally, choose carry-on luggage that's as lightweight as possible but still durable. While leather bags look great, they're heavier and more expensive than bags constructed of synthetic materials such as nylon or polyester, which are the lightest. For nylons and polyester, the thickness of the fibers, or "denier," generally determines its durability, says Jean Noe Clark in *Consumers Digest.* Typically, the higher the denier, the stronger the fiber. According to Clark, many premium

# TRAVEL FITNESS TIPS: PACKING FOR A WORKOUT

Leaving home without your exercise gear makes it almost certain that you won't work out. Now that you have a game plan for fitness, what athletic wear should you pack? Here are some tips from fitness pros and veteran travelers.

- Pack what you need to meet your exercise goals. If, for example, you've opted to work out in your hotel room, consider packing an exercise videotape, jump rope, exercise tubing, or light weights to increase your exercise choices. Avoid packing heavy "travel gyms," like 10-pound portable stepping machines or other cumbersome equipment. You can always use the hotel stairs as your Stairmaster.

- For travel to a warm climate, pack lightweight, loose-fitting, 100 percent cotton shorts, T-shirts and other exercise clothing that allows perspiration to evaporate. Bring along sunscreen to protect yourself from harmful ultraviolet radiation.

- For travel to a cold climate, pack clothing that can be easily layered if you plan to exercise outdoors. For example, pack cotton sweats, a long-sleeved cotton shirt, windbreaker, hat, and gloves for running or fitness walking. Watch for overpacking. Overdressing for cold-weather exercise is a common mistake. Remember that even an average workout can make the temperature feel 30 degrees warmer.

- Whenever possible, reduce what exercise gear you carry. For example, Jim Topinka, 47, regularly travels from his home in San Francisco to Washington, DC and leaves a set of exercise and swim clothes at the hotel where he always stays so he doesn't have to pack them every time. Also, many hotels provide workout clothes to guests. Find out what your hotel has available before packing your bag.

- Pack a good pair of walking shoes. Even for a one-day trip, be prepared to do some brisk walking.

carry-ons are made from ballistic nylon (over 1,000 denier) which is so strong that perforations do not tear the fabric. However, luggage made from 420-denier nylon or 600-denier polyester provides sufficient durability for most travelers. Business travel expert George Albert Brown, author of *The Airline Passenger's Guerrilla Handbook* (1989), recommends a nylon garment bag and small nylon boarding bag as the perfect carry-on combination. When choosing a boarding bag, consider the rectangular carry-ons with wheels and a retractable rigid handle for hauling the bag through airports. With the self-contained rolling bag, you don't have to fuss with strapping your luggage into a portable carrying cart and run the risk of having a suitcase tumble out as you round a corner.

If, despite your best efforts to cut back what you carry, you still need to check bags, choose soft-sided luggage which is more lightweight. The lightest soft-sided bag can weigh as little as 1-1/2 to 2-1/2 pounds, while a hard-sided suitcase can weigh 10 to 20 pounds empty. Choose a bag with wheels or use an airport luggage cart to avoid straining yourself. When you must check bags, always pack one carry-on with basic necessities such as your passport, traveler's checks, keys, tickets, medicine, and toiletries. That way, if your bags are en route to Poughkeepsie while you stare blankly at the luggage carousel in Portland, you can still survive.

Packing fit requires more than traveling light. You also need to pack with comfort as a priority. Whether you're traveling by car, plane, bus, or train, make sure to bring loose, non-restricting, comfortable clothing to wear in transit. There's nothing worse than wearing tightly cinched clothing during a long flight or drive. Keep comfort in mind when you're packing your professional garb as well. You'll just feel better and get around easier in light, non-restrictive clothing. Debbie Wloch, 33, an investment banker from Chicago, packs what she refers to as her "traveling suits." "These are the ones that I can maneuver in easily. The skirts are not too tight or too long so I can get in and out of cabs and airplanes. I only pack looser clothes," she says.

As you build your travel health and fitness program, you'll discover that packing certain items is essential to meeting your fitness goals. As you read *Travel Fitness*, note fitness items to pack in the future. Make a list to check before each trip, keeping in mind specific travel fitness goals or use the list we have provided. What items will prepare you to cope with the flight? Combat stress? Sleep better? Take advantage of athletic opportunities? Consider having a satchel of indispensable fitness items packed and ready to go on a moment's notice. After all, preparation is the key to your travel fitness success.

# *Travel Fitness Tips: The Fit Traveler's Packing List*

Here are some ideas of things to take along. Mind you, we're not recommending that you pack them all. Peruse the list for items that might be particularly helpful in meeting your travel fitness goals. Add or subtract items to make this list right for you. Some of the suggestions may make more sense as you read further in the book.

## 1. For Well-Being

- ❏ sport belt
- ❏ lumbar roll
- ❏ inflatable neck rest/pillow
- ❏ eye shades
- ❏ ear plugs
- ❏ nasal spray
- ❏ eye drops
- ❏ slippers or thick socks (to wear on the plane)

- ❏ good moisturizer
- ❏ travel humidifier
- ❏ sunscreen
- ❏ water spritzer
- ❏ lip balm
- ❏ _____
- ❏ _____
- ❏ _____

## 2. For In Transit/Downtime Entertainment

- ❏ a good novel
- ❏ audio books
- ❏ music tapes
- ❏ magazines
- ❏ guidebooks
- ❏ travel faxes/software

- ❏ small cassette player
- ❏ electronic games
- ❏ _____
- ❏ _____
- ❏ _____

## 3. For Diet

- ❏ bottled water
- ❏ raw bran
- ❏ small boxes of raisins, soda crackers, tea, and other snacks
- ❏ immersion heater
- ❏ metal spoon

- ❏ rigid plastic cup
- ❏ fat gram, sodium, cholesterol, and/or calorie counter
- ❏ _____
- ❏ _____
- ❏ _____

## 4. For Fitness

- ❏ athletic bag
- ❏ weight-lifting gloves
- ❏ walking/running shoes, cross trainers
- ❏ loose-fitting exercise clothes (layers in winter, light in summer)
- ❏ plenty of white socks

- ❏ ankle weights
- ❏ other portable workout gear
- ❏ personal travel exercise routine
- ❏ music and music player
- ❏ exercise audiotape/ videotape
- ❏ pedometer

- ❑ swimming gear (even if only for the Jacuzzi/sauna)
- ❑ jump rope
- ❑ exercise bands/surgical tubing
- ❑ water weights
- ❑ wrist weights
- ❑ sports bra, jock strap
- ❑ plastic bag for dirty athletic clothes
- ❑ _____
- ❑ _____
- ❑ _____

### 5. For Emotional Comfort

- ❑ family photo
- ❑ your own pillow
- ❑ comforting things from home (like pjs)
- ❑ relaxation tapes
- ❑ security lock
- ❑ travel alarm clock
- ❑ _____
- ❑ _____
- ❑ _____

### 6. For Emergencies

- ❑ medication and copies of prescriptions
- ❑ multi-purpose antibiotic, diarrhea medication (for international travel)
- ❑ sports injury first aid kit
- ❑ _____
- ❑ _____
- ❑ _____

### 7. For Planning

- ❑ the *Airline Seating Guide*
- ❑ the *Official Airline Guide*
- ❑ detailed itinerary (including contingency travel plans)
- ❑ list of key information (including important telephone numbers, names of overseas doctors)
- ❑ _____
- ❑ _____
- ❑ _____

# International Fitness Planning

Fitness planning is never more important than for international travel. Don't be caught off guard if your itinerary takes you away from clearly safe destinations like London, Paris, or Tokyo to lesser-known spots in Asia, Africa, or South America. Traveling to the tropics, high-altitude locations, and less developed countries requires specialized planning just to stay healthy, let alone feel fit. If malaria or yellow fever is a threat, just getting all the right vaccinations and pills in order can take two to three months.

For travel to less developed countries or trips lasting three weeks or longer, most experts recommend a trip or telephone call to a travel medicine specialist, *not* your family physician. You're going to need expert guidance. Ask the specialist to assess your health, give you tips for avoiding health problems, and prescribe necessary and recommended vaccinations and medications. Make sure that your routine vaccines are up-to-date, too. Tetanus, polio, rubella, diphtheria, and other diseases eradicated in the West are still lurking in much of the Third World. Stock up on enough medications to last the entire trip, and take along prescriptions just in case. Most travelers take along an antibiotic and anti-diarrheal medication to handle the two-step.

Also request that the physician analyze your itinerary and planned physical activities in detail. Any competent travel medicine specialist should give you strategies for avoiding problems from heat, altitude, and contaminated food and water. After all, staying healthy abroad requires more than the right medication: it also depends on smart behavior. If you're eating street food, imbibing tap water or iced drinks, or munching raw fruits and salads, you're probably going to get sick despite taking pills to ward off diarrhea. (For tips on staying healthy while eating abroad, refer to Chapter 6). Similarly, if you're traveling to the tropics, where malaria is endemic, using mosquito repellent, wearing long sleeves, and staying only in accommodations with air conditioning or screens is the best medicine because no preventive medication is 100 percent effective.

Most major universities have travel medicine clinics which are a good place to start your international fitness planning. While a competent travel medicine doctor is an invaluable resource, remember that you have the primary responsibility to keep yourself healthy and fit while abroad. Will your medical insurance cover you for injuries or illness while abroad? Can you fill your prescriptions at your destination? How will you find a competent doctor in a Third World country? These are just some of the many questions to ask yourself before taking off.

We suggest that you contact at least one of the resources listed in the following **Resources for International Travelers** guide (p. 14) to gather information before consulting a physician. With research in hand, you'll know what questions to ask the doctor and have a head start in developing a game plan for handling sickness or injury while abroad. Make an effort also to obtain the names of one or two reliable English-speaking physicians at your destination. Confirm with your insurance company that any medical expenses will be covered while traveling. Many travelers unnecessarily purchase supplemental medical coverage when they were already covered under their own policy.

# Resources for International Travelers

Listed below are organizations providing resources of particular interest to international travelers. Whether you need a list of recommended vaccines, a safety report, or a cultural profile of a particular country, one of the organizations here will be able to help.

**International Association for Medical Assistance to Travelers (IAMAT)**
**417 Center Street**
**Lewiston, NY 14092**                                     **(716) 754-4883**

This nonprofit agency provides a veritable gold mine of materials to international travelers, such as a directory of American and English-speaking doctors in 500 cities around the world; specific guidelines on malaria and other tropical diseases; up-to-date health information, including data on the safety of food and water; and world climate and immunization charts. Membership is free.

**U.S. Centers for Disease Control (CDC)**
**Fax Information Service**                                **(404) 332-4565**

CDC offers faxed international traveler health information, including traveler's diarrhea and food and water precautions, disease risk and prevention tips by region, outbreak bulletins, HIV/AIDS information, and other government-recommended precautions.

**CDC International Traveler's Hotline**
**(404) 639-2572/(404) 332-4559**

For the cost of a phone call, CDC provides prerecorded information on geographic-specific vaccination requirements and recommendations, food and water precautions, tips for avoiding traveler's diarrhea, reports on specific disease outbreaks, and information on HIV/AIDS and foreign travel. Published material is also available, including CDC's annual book, *Health Information for International Travel.*

**U.S. State Department, Overseas Citizens' Emergency Center**
**Washington, DC**                                         **(202) 647-5225**

The center provides medical, legal, and other assistance to Americans abroad, information on current epidemics and health conditions, travel warnings, and consular information sheets.

**U.S. State Department**
**Washington, DC**
**Consular Affairs, Automated Fax Service: (202) 647-3000**
**For information via computer: (202) 647-9225**

This office provides free information sheets on specific foreign countries.

**International SOS Assistance**
**P.O. Box 11568**
**Philadelphia, PA 19116          (215) 245-4707/(800) 523-8930**

SOS offers 24-hour medical, personal, and travel assistance, including pre-trip medical referral information, 24-hour worldwide medical information and assistance, emergency medication information, emergency evacuation, and access to emergency assistance centers throughout the world. For $40, individuals can purchase an SOS membership for trips lasting up to 14 days.

**Travel Health Fax                          (800) 777-7751**

Shoreland Medical Marketing, Inc. offers three- to four-page faxes with complete up-to-the-minute profiles on individual countries, including information on immunization and visa requirements, health "dos and don'ts," climate, geography, altitude, air quality, and safety. Cost: $10, first country; $6, each additional request.

**Immunization Alert                          (800) 584-1999**

This service provides computerized "trip reports," including travel health information and complete reports on individual countries. Cost: $10, first country; $5, each additional request.

**Global Emergency Medical Services, Inc.**
**2001 Westside Drive, Suite 120**
**Alpharetta, GA 30201                          (800) 860-1111**

Global Emergency Medical Services, Inc. offers comprehensive health prevention, intervention, and monitoring services to international travelers. Services include 24-hour access to a health line staffed by registered nurses, and a complete directory of medical care providers, clinics, and hospitals tailored to a traveler's itinerary. Cost: $250 for an annual subscription.

**Brigham Young University                          (800) 528-6279**

BYU publishes "Culturgrams," four-page briefings on specific foreign countries, including local customs, greetings, general attitude, holidays, history, culture, lifestyle, transportation, health, and travel requirements. Cost: $3.00, first Culturgram; $1.50, additional requests.

Before departing, make a checklist of what you'll need to go abroad, including vaccination certificates, prescriptions, and medications. Keep all of your health documents in one file.

If you become sick once abroad, you can call the local American Embassy or Consulate for a referral to an English-speaking physician or access to reliable sources of medication. For medical help, don't forget your credit card. American Express card's Global Assist Hotline at (800) 554-AMEX and Diner's Club card, Club Assistance, at (800) 346-3779 will help you find an English-speaking physician and direct you to treatment. Of course, the hotel doctor and local hospital are possibilities.

Planning also is crucial to lessen the stress of culture shock. Bone up on the history, customs, and culture of your destination before leaving. The more you know about the place, the less anxious you'll feel there. Guidebooks, travel articles, and on-line computer travel information services are a start. But when you need to dig a little deeper, call a university with a respected language department for expert advice, ask questions of co-workers or friends who have been there, or someone working in your company's branch office located there. Contact the foreign country's embassy in the United States, or find a travel agent that specializes in the area.

It can be challenging to work out in another country. For tips on exercising while abroad, refer to Chapter 5.

The remaining chapters in this book tackle the primary fitness concerns you, as a traveler, have on the road. From diet to jet lag, stress to exercise, sleep to flying fit, the best tips and strategies for coping with travel are on the pages that follow. So keep reading to find out how you can feel better the next time you're away from home.

# The Travel Health and Fitness Itinerary Checklist

❑ Identify and prioritize fitness areas you want to improve.

❑ Write down your goals and review them before and during each trip.

❑ Always travel light.

❑ Pack around one color scheme.

❑ Pack clothes that serve more than one function.

❑ Limit the number of shoes you bring.

❑ Wear your athletic shoes on the plane.

❑ Use travel sizes.

❑ Call ahead to find out what amenities your hotel offers.

❑ Use lightweight luggage.

❑ Pack loose, comfortable clothes.

❑ Pack to accommodate your specific health and fitness goals.

❑ If you're traveling to a less developed country or abroad for an extended stay, contact a travel medicine specialist.

# Health and Fitness in Transit

*"You define a good flight by negatives: you didn't get hijacked, you didn't crash, you didn't throw up, you weren't late, you weren't nauseated by the food. So you are grateful."*

Paul Theroux
*The Old Patagonian Express*

**H**ow do you feel after a five-hour flight or long car drive? Chances are, pretty lousy. Whether you routinely brave those less-than-friendly skies, or cruise by bus like John Madden, or travel by car or train, simply getting there poses a formidable fitness challenge.

So many factors, from cattle-car seating to poor air quality and fatty food, conspire to rob you of your energy and well-being. You can, however, meet this ultimate fitness challenge by following a few simple guidelines.

To improve your chances of arriving fit and alert, you first need to learn how getting there affects the body. This chapter addresses the stresses of air and car travel, and tells you how to take charge of your health in transit.

# Air Conditions

If you've ever felt headachy, tired, or disoriented after a long flight, you're not alone. Most frequent air travelers experience some level of physical and mental lassitude and usually attribute it to jet lag, the disruption of internal body rhythms caused by crossing multiple time zones. But jet lag is only part of the story. Even if you never cross a time zone while flying, your body is still challenged by the partially pressurized cabin environment, nearly bereft of humidity and skimpy on fresh air.

Within minutes of take-off, you're whisked to an effective altitude as much as 1-1/2 times the height of Denver. That's because the cabin is pressurized to simulate an altitude of 5,000 to 8,000 feet, although the plane itself may be cruising at 25,000 to 40,000 feet.

Ideally, the cabin would be pressurized at sea level, but this would cause weight and structural problems. To simulate an altitude of 5,000 to 8,000 feet during the flight, the aircraft's engines continuously pull outside air into the cabin. As the air is brought in and then cooled, almost every bit of humidity is wrung out. Outlet valves then create the desired pressure by regulating the volume of air in the cabin. The specific cabin pressure does vary somewhat by aircraft. For example, the Boeing 747 typically simulates a lower altitude (4,700 feet) while the McDonnell Douglas DC-9 typically simulates a higher altitude (8,000 feet).

At higher altitudes, there's a decrease in atmospheric pressure and a corresponding decrease in available oxygen. If you're in a DC-9, your body experiences a 33 percent decrease in ambient oxygen concentration. In a 747, your body experiences a 17 percent drop in available oxygen. The decreased pressure causes gases to expand. That's why the potato chip and peanut bags served on the plane look like they're about to burst. Your body tissues also fill up with these expanding gases, making your shoes seem two sizes too small.

What are the effects on the airborne traveler? If you're otherwise healthy, your body will adjust to the altitude change, but not without some stress. For starters, your heart and lungs must work harder to process what oxygen is there. For many, the stress is like walking fast and may cause mild hypoxia. "A prolonged flight at maximum altitude is going to increase the degree of fatigue you're going to feel," says Dr. John P. McCann, regional flight surgeon for United Airlines.

Because optimal functioning depends on the body's ability to take in high levels of oxygen, travelers may experience hangover-like symptoms which researchers have dubbed the "in-flight syndrome." The symptoms include dizziness, fatigue, headaches, tunnel vision, nausea, or tingling in the hands and feet that can last a day or more. Your brain may be working less optimally as well. Researchers have demonstrated that decreased oxygen concentrations at cabin altitude can impair the ability to learn new tasks in otherwise healthy people. Meanwhile, your circulatory system is busy trying to eliminate trapped gases. The result: a certain amount of hemodynamic stress at take-off and landing. Add to that dehydration from extremely low cabin humidity and you have a real assault on your cells.

Airlines have also greatly reduced the influx of fresh air on newer planes, compounding the body's burden. Many older planes built before the mid-1980s offer 100 percent fresh air which is completely changed every three minutes. To save on fuel costs for cooling the air coming into the ventilation systems through the engines, newer models like the MD-80 have only 50 percent fresh air and 50 percent recirculated air which is changed every six to seven minutes. The recirculated air is filtered through high-efficiency "hospital" filters. While the cockpit receives 100 percent fresh air, ventilation rates vary within the passenger cabins. The ventilation rate per passenger in first-class may be two to three times higher than in coach. One flight attendants' union contends that the crews on some sparsely filled flights cut the fresh air intake even more to save on fuel.

Experts disagree on the effects of such low levels of fresh air in a confined space, but there is concern about the risk of exposure to higher levels of carbon dioxide, fumes, toxic chemicals used to build and clean aircraft, germs, and other contaminants. Tobacco smoke on international flights poses an added risk. "On longer flights you might notice more rapid breathing, burning eyes, blocked noses, tingling feet and hands, headaches, or nausea if the air quality is poor," says Andy D. Yates, Jr., a former pilot with United Airlines for 42 years and chairman of the Air Transport Medicine Committee of the Aerospace Medical Association.

A 1989 Department of Transportation study of cabin air quality showed relatively high carbon dioxide levels, low cabin humidity, and cosmic radiation exposure on 92 randomly selected flights. Many flight attendants, and some passengers, blame their health problems on poor cabin air. Some feel so disoriented after a flight that they reportedly can't even dial a phone. But the airlines and manufacturers say cabin air quality is better than that in most office buildings.

Because of the increasing number of complaints reported by passengers, the Transportation Department and the Centers for Disease Control are looking into air quality in newer planes. The CDC is particularly concerned about four cases where tuberculosis may have been spread to passengers.

How healthy is the air inside your car on a long-distance trip? In part, it depends on outside environmental conditions but, unlike air travel, you do have some control over the air quality in your car. For example, rolling the windows down creates an influx of fresh air into the car. If, however, the outdoor air is polluted, closing the windows and turning on the air conditioner or vents buffers outside pollutants or allergens. According to one study, particle levels measured inside test vehicles were always lower than levels outside when the air conditioning or vents were open and the windows were closed.

Auto heating, ventilation, and air conditioning (HVAC) systems typically offer two air intake options: outside air (OSA) and recirculated air (RECIRC). Drivers can choose either option in using the HVAC system. OSA rapidly changes interior air, promoting fresh air in the car, and is generally a good option for maintaining high-level interior air quality. OSA also helps remove interior moisture, keeping the windows clear, and is recommended for all heating situations. RECIRC reduces the amount of outside air getting into your car. Consequently, it limits some odor and particles from entering the vehicle. If you're navigating a congested freeway in Los Angeles during a smog alert, RECIRC might be a better bet to inhibit outside air pollutants from entering your car. If you're traveling through the countryside of Vermont, however, OSA is a good option (unless you're allergic to pollen).

To make the air inside of cars healthier, some manufacturers have added special filters to new cars that capture annoying allergens, fumes, and smog. But car air conditioners, filters, and intake ducts themselves can be a source of microbial and other particles, especially in older cars.

Certainly, you can't spend your next flight or drive worrying about bad air, communicable diseases, and cosmic radiation. These matters are mostly out of your control. But there are some simple steps you can take to meet the challenges of travel. Your first line of defense is to combat dehydration.

# Traversing the Sahara

If you ventured by camel across the Sahara without water, guzzling beer and munching salty peanuts, you probably would succumb to dehydration long before reaching your destination. What you may not realize is that cabin air is drier than the Sahara; yet few travelers take any precautions to prevent dehydration. In fact, they aggravate the problem with alcohol and sodium.

The humidity in most planes typically ranges from 8 to 12 percent, but can drop as low as 2 percent. The longer the flight, the drier it gets. That's because at cruising altitude the humidity outside is almost zero. When outside air is brought in through the engines and cooled, any remaining humidity is removed. Most of the humidity is actually from the sweat and breath of your traveling companions.

The unwary flier can lose up to two pounds of water in a three-hour flight. Car travelers also wind up dehydrated because they stop drinking fluids to avoid "pit stops." Dehydration causes your cells to become less efficient, contributing to fatigue and poor performance. "Water is a forgotten nutrient," writes Robert K. Cooper, Ph.D., in *Health and Fitness Excellence* (1989). "It takes surprisingly little fluid loss—1 percent—for your body to become dehydrated, and you can't depend on thirst to tell you that it's happening."

As your cells dry out, they pull water from your blood, reducing your blood volume. Your heart pumps harder trying to circulate the smaller volume of blood to every part of your body. The thickened blood is less able to whisk oxygen and nutrients to muscles and to eliminate wastes, making you feel tired, even lightheaded, dizzy, and headachy. You also may be more apt to catch your fellow passengers' colds or other airborne diseases because of dry respiratory passages, according to some experts.

The simplest way to beat dehydration is to drink—*water*, that is, and lots of it. It's best not to rely on thirst to gauge your dehydration level; thirst reliably underestimates your body's true need for water. Experts recommend increasing fluid intake before boarding the plane, and gulping at least one 8-ounce glass of water for every hour in flight. If you're traveling by car, keep water accessible and drink at least six to eight cups every day.

Flight attendants suggest avoiding the water from the plane's holding tank, which they say is treated with chlorine and other chemicals, but rarely changed. "It's like drinking from a swimming pool," says one veteran flight attendant. There's even more reason to avoid the plane's water—including ice cubes—on international flights from Third World countries where contamination is more of an issue. To ensure a good drink, you might tote your own bottled water on board, but many airlines now offer spring water. If you haven't thought ahead or don't want the hassle of packing water, you can buy good water at most airports or fill up your own plastic quart container before boarding.

While water or fruit juices help to hydrate you, stay away from beverages with caffeine, including coffee, tea, and soft drinks, and limit your consumption of alcohol. "All of these increase diuresis, the elimination of fluids from the body," says Eric Sternlicht, associate professor of physiology at Occidental College in Los Angeles and a recognized authority on exercise and nutrition.

Remember, altitude increases the effects of alcohol, so it's best to be a teetotaler en route. And carbonated beverages, even Perrier, can cause discomfort as gas expands in your body. Dr. Sternlicht also recommends avoiding those ubiquitous salt-laden peanuts and pretzel snacks served by the airlines and salty drinks like tomato juice, which add to dehydration.

What to do about those sore, red eyes, parched skin, and dry sinuses? Try using saline eye drops during and after a flight, especially if you wear contacts. Apply a good moisturizer every hour or two to exposed skin and lip balm to your lips. Some inveterate travelers carry a water spritzer and spray their face and hair every so often. Frequent flier Steve Campbell, 51, of Seattle, whose hectic schedule has kept him traveling from the United States to the Far East as often as six times a month, periodically visits the lavatory to pat his face with a wet paper towel. To relieve sinuses, many travelers use a nasal spray before takeoff and a nasal cream in-flight. You might even ask for a warm towel, place it over your nose and mouth and breath through it. One old flight attendant trick: drink hot water with lemon. The steam moistens dry sinuses, and the warmth stimulates your digestive system to work better.

## Dress for Fitness

Scrunched in an airplane or car seat for hours on end, you certainly don't need to be wearing a noose-like tie, panty hose that feel like tourniquets, or not-so-sensible dress shoes.

"I can't understand why people dress up to fly. There's nobody to impress," says frequent traveler Randy Petersen, 40, of Colorado

Springs, who logs about 500,000 air miles a year. "I used to sit there all dressed up at 30,000 feet. Then I asked myself, Why am I doing this? What's the protocol here? Now I only travel in comfortable clothing."

If you'll be traveling any distance, dress in loose-fitting, athletic clothing. Consider dressing in layers to acclimate to the changing cabin temperatures. On transoceanic flights, Steve Campbell even packs Chinese slippers for warmth and comfort just in case he is seated next to an emergency door with an insulation gap.

There's even less reason to dress up if you'll just be checking into a hotel room after a trip. Many frequent travelers who will face a business meeting at the end of the journey leave in work clothes, but pack sweats or other comfortable clothing in a carry-on gym bag. Just before boarding, they change in the airport restroom. That way, their work clothes don't get crumpled during the flight, and they can stretch, exercise, and catnap with ease. After landing, they change again.

# Location, Location, Location

"They treat us like sardines" is a common lament of frequent fliers, referring to the cattle-car seating on most airlines. In a 1991 survey of air travelers by *Consumer Reports*, respondents rated airplane seating as the factor causing greatest distress. No wonder. Being crammed into a seat that barely reclines and has limited legroom creates a nightmare for anyone—especially on transcontinental and international flights. But with a little knowledge and advance planning, you can find yourself a roomy seat.

## *Lesson One: The Airlines Decide How Much Room You Get*

Seat comfort depends on the distance between seat rows (creating legroom), seat width (creating space between the armrests), and seat groupings within a row (determining your chances of having neighbors on one or both sides). It's not up to the aircraft manufacturers to decide seat arrangements. Each airline determines how many seats to cram into a plane, and most periodically reconfigure their aircraft. The same type of aircraft may have a different number of seats, depending on the airline. So it pays to choose your carrier wisely.

The *Consumer Reports Travel Letter's* 1993 survey of U.S. airline coach seating ranked Midwest Express, TWA, and UltrAir very high in seating comfort. TWA recently increased the space between coach seats from 31 to 36 inches. Even given the differences among airlines, the 767 airplane scored the highest in comfort of any aircraft. (See accompanying table to see how other aircraft fared). *Consumer Reports* also noted that airlines increasingly use 757s and 737s instead of wide-body jets for flights of 2,000 miles or more, creating a comfort disaster for passengers. These planes offer narrower seats and a higher chance of being stuck in or next to a middle seat.

## *Lesson Two: All Seats Are Not Created Equal*

No matter what the airplane's seating configuration, some seats will be roomier than others. Most savvy travelers always book an aisle seat. Window seats scrunch your shoulder and arm on the window side, and middle seats place you between two seatmates of unknown size and temperament. With an aisle seat, you can extend your legroom to the aisle by sticking your legs out and only risk proximity to one seatmate.

Bulkhead seats, behind cabin dividers, are highly coveted by comfort-seekers. They offer extra legroom and nobody in front of you. But there are some big drawbacks: no storage under the seat, difficulty viewing the movie, and the chance of screaming kids nearby (some airlines reserve the first row or two of coach for passengers with children).

Seats in emergency exit rows and behind midcabin doors also offer extra legroom. If you can, opt for the emergency exit rows: they're quiet and roomier and offer storage under the seat. You also can opt to board early to "study" safety instructions. The door row seats, conversely, may be noisy because they tend to be near the lavatories or galleys, both high-traffic areas.

Sometimes sitting right by the window over the wing in coach offers more legroom at no extra charge. On many planes, airlines eliminate the window seats that are over the wing to expedite passage out of the aircraft during an emergency. The result: the seat behind the one removed has extra legroom. Consider asking for this coveted seat the next time you make reservations.

Remember, seats in the last row of a section generally don't recline and seats in front of exit rows don't recline fully, if at all. On an international flight where smoking is still allowed, avoid the "transition section" between smoking and nonsmoking. Otherwise, you may inhale as much second-hand smoke as your fellow passengers in the smoking section. Also, avoid sitting on the sunny side of the aircraft, especially if you intend to catch some shut-eye.

## Squeezing the Sardines

| Plane | Seat width[a] | Configuration[b] | Impaired comfort[c] |
|---|---|---|---|
| A300[d] | 20 | 2-4-2 | 18% |
| | 18.5 | 3-3-3[e] | 50 |
| A320 | 20 | 3-3 | 50 |
| DC9/MD80[f] | 20 | 2-3 | 21 |
| | 22 | 2-2[g] | 0 |
| DC10/MD11 | 20 | 2-5-2 | 20 |
| | 18.5 | 3-4-3[e] | 46 |
| | 21 | 2-2-2-2[g] | 0 |
| F100/200 | 20 | 2-3 | 21 |
| L1011 | 20 | 2-5-2 | 20 |
| | 18.5 | 3-4-3[e] | 46 |
| 727 | 19 | 3-3 | 50 |
| | 22 | 2-3[g] | 21 |
| 737 | 19 | 3-3 | 50 |
| 747 | 19.5 | 3-4-3 | 46 |
| 757 | 19 | 3-3 | 50 |
| 767 | 19 | 2-3-2 | 15 |

NOTE: All data apply to Coach/Economy seating.
[a]In inches, measured between armrest centers.
[b]As used by most scheduled airlines, except as noted.
[c]Refers to the percentage of travelers whose comfort is impaired by sitting in a middle seat or next to someone in an occupied seat, when airline's average occupancy factor is 70 percent.
[d]Includes A310, A330, A340.
[e]Undesirable charter configuration; also used by a few scheduled airlines.
[f]Includes MD81, 82, 83, 87, 88.
[g]Desirable nonstandard ("premium") Coach/Economy configuration, used by a few small airlines.

Note. From "Snug seats in the sky—Avoiding the coach crunch." Copyright 1993 by Consumers Union of the U.S., Inc., Yonkers, NY, 10703-1057. Adapted by permission from *Consumer Reports Travel Letter*, July 1993.

## *Lesson Three: Any Seat Is Better If the One Beside It Is Empty*

A vacant seat next to you goes a long way to improve comfort. There are some tricks to improving the odds of sitting next to an empty seat. Frequent fliers say that seats in the middle section of wide-body planes are mostly avoided. If you request the aisle seat in the middle section, your chances of having an empty seat beside you are higher. What's more, if you're traveling with a companion, ask for the aisle and the window seat in a three-seat row. Because airlines routinely fill aisle and window seats first, the seat between you won't be assigned unless the plane fills up. If all else fails, wait until just before the door closes, and scan for open seats. If you find space, make your move. Says veteran flight attendant Joyce Scardina from San Francisco: "If you can find space in coach, it makes for a better flight. You can stretch out and relax. But don't wait for a flight attendant to help you—they won't."

## Lesson Four: First Class Offers More Than Snob Appeal

If you're in first class, you'll board first and leave first, minimizing stress. Even better, the seats on the average are seven inches deeper and three inches wider than they are in coach. Dr. Sternlicht advises upgrading to first class whenever possible. "That way you have room to move around and aren't so cramped. There's also better access to fluids," he says.

As we've said before, you also just might breathe easier—literally. First class passengers get more fresh air per cubic foot because the population is less dense. Even on overbooked flights, there's often a good chance to upgrade because a number of first-class passengers opt to be bumped in exchange for free tickets, leaving space in first class.

## Lesson Five: A Little Advance Planning Goes a Long Way

An obscure publication called *The Airline Seating Guide*, published by six-foot-one-inch Monty Stanford, is a good place to start. The guide informs travelers which seats are the roomiest; which have an airfone; which recline; which letters indicate aisle, window, and middle seats; which seats are close to the smoking section; and more. Start by asking the ticket agent what type of aircraft will be used on the flight; get the most specific designation of equipment as possible. Then, consult the guide to choose the best seat. The guide is available from Carlson Publishing Co., Box 888, Los Alamitos, CA 90720, (310) 493-4877, for $39.95 a year for the U.S. edition, $44.95 a year for the overseas edition. The *Official Airline Guide* (OAG), published by Official Airline Guides, 2000 Clearwater Drive, Oakbrook, IL 60521, (800) 323-4000, is available in many travel agencies and corporate travel offices. It also provides seating charts for domestic and international carriers. If you don't want the hassle of charting your own seat, have your travel or airline ticket agent pull up the plane's configuration on the reservation screen and help you book the best possible seat.

## Surviving Your Seat

Whether you travel by car, plane, bus, or train, there's no escaping a good deal of sitting on any trip. But the way you choose to sit will affect your back, energy level, and general well-being. Sitting for any length of time challenges the back because it creates more compressive force on the discs than any other posture and limits the nutrient-rich blood supply to the back. The problem is that airplane seats and many car seats are not well designed and actually encourage a contorted, slumping posture, which leads to fatigue, stiffness, and even pain in the neck and back. Those one-size-fits-all airplane seats, complete with ill-fitting headrests and too-narrow seats, are particularly incompatible with the natural contours of your body, says Charlie Longdon, exercise physiologist at the St. Francis Hospital Spine Center in San Francisco. "Airplane seats are notorious because their design doesn't support the lumbar back," says Longdon. "It takes too much effort to sit up in them, so people slouch instead, decreasing the optimal alignment of the back." Even a one-hour flight can put you at risk for neck and back pain, sore muscles, fatigue, and eye strain. The longer the journey, and the more you travel, the worse off you'll be.

To avoid in-transit back and neck distress, try some of these tips:

- *Practice "dynamic sitting."* This is a form of active sitting, using full skeletal support, writes David Zemach-Bersin in *Relaxercise* (1990), a book based on the work of Dr. Moshe Feldenkrais. The idea is to properly align yourself so that your skeleton, not your muscles and ligaments, supports your body. "When your muscles and ligaments are doing the work that your skeleton should be doing, they become tense, over-used, and strained. Even if your muscles are large and strong, your bones are capable of supporting your body's weight with far greater efficiency," writes Zemach-Bersin. The key to dynamic sitting is using your pelvic sitting bones as your body's main source of support. To achieve pelvic support, slightly arch your lower back and distribute your weight evenly over your pelvic bones. Don't cross your legs; it shifts weight to your lower back and can cause pain. Also, do

# PICKING A COMFORTABLE RENTAL OR COMPANY CAR

From a health and fitness standpoint, the principal consideration in choosing a rental or company car for business travel is seat comfort. Many car seats, because of their poor design, can be challenging to the back. In fact, the type of car you drive correlates to back pain, notes Robert K. Cooper in *Health and Fitness Excellence*. "Motorists driving cars with poor-quality seats faced three times the risk of developing lower back problems over drivers of many Swedish and Japanese cars," writes Cooper, who believes proper seating is vital to health and reaction time when driving.

To be comfortable for long periods of time, a car seat should accommodate the driver's size, shape, and changing positions and reduce postural stress, says Mac Reynolds, a professor of biomechanics at Michigan State University. Before choosing a company or rental car, Reynolds suggests looking for the following features affecting seat comfort:

- **Six-way power seat adjustments.** Look for seats that adjust for horizontal distance from the controls (forward/back), height (up/down), and back angle (tilt). Newer cars offer adjusting seat cushions as well. Being able to define the best seat position for you is critical to comfort.

- **Contour.** Avoid highly contoured seats. They may look great, but they're not comfortable to sit in because they don't accommodate for differences in people or make it easy to change positions. Look for firm seats with gentle contours that support you across a variety of tasks.

- **Posture support.** Look for a seat design that supports proper posture. Proper sitting entails using your pelvic bones for support. Reynolds suggests that you ask yourself the following question when you're "test-driving" potential rental or company cars. As you sit in the car, can you position your buttocks into the area where the bottom cushion and seat back meet, without sliding out or feeling pressure there?

If you can, the seat design supports proper posture. Some seats, however, have design structures that create a hard region where the seat back meets the cushion, making it difficult to maintain proper posture.

- **Lumbar support.** Finding proper lumbar support in the seat back is tricky business, says Reynolds. In many cars, the lumbar support is a "one-size-fits-all" proposition. Depending on your size and the design of the seat, the built-in lumbar support may be pressing your back in the wrong spot, causing discomfort. Only expensive cars offer forward/back *and* up/down adjustments to lumbar support. The up/down adjustment allows for proper placement of the lumbar support along the spine, thereby accommodating differing sizes and shapes.

- **Absorbent materials.** The worst fate for any long-distance driver is moisture accumulating on the seat. Look for porous seat materials that will transfer water vapor through the seat. Choose cloth over leather seats—they breathe easier. Many leather seats are coated with preservatives which prevent water vapors from being absorbed into the seat.

- **Space.** Does the car offer sufficient physical and psychological space? Choose a large enough car. Sitting in cramped quarters with your head pressed against the car ceiling won't add pleasure to any trip.

Other features also affect driver and passenger comfort. Cruise control and tilt steering increase postural comfort, and air conditioning is absolutely necessary.

---

what truck drivers long ago discovered: keep your wallet out of your back pocket. Amazingly, one study (Gould, N., 1974, *New England Journal of Medicine*) showed that chronic back pain diminished for many men once they stopped sitting on their wallets. Keep your shoulders and abdomen relaxed, and slightly arch your neck. On the plane, if you're using a laptop, don't rest it on your lap; place it on pillows or the tray so you don't bend over too far. If you're driving, only tense those muscles you're using to drive. Keep your shoulders, back, and neck relaxed. Keep breathing!

- *Create your comfort.* Your first goal is to support your spine's natural curves and to keep your neck and shoulders relaxed. Ellen Hollander takes a sausage-shaped, down-filled pillow on every trip which she uses to support her lower back. There also are inflatable lumbar rolls on the market and ergonomically designed cushions for your car that support your back while you drive. Those car seat covers made of wooden beads don't help support your back but they do stimulate circulation, inhibit moisture accumulation, and keep you cooler, according to Dr. Donald R. McLoughlin, a chiropractor in the Los Angeles area. If you don't pack lumbar support, grab a pillow from a flight attendant, or roll a blanket and place it in the crook of your back.

  Many travelers won't leave home without their inflatable, wrap-around neck pillows. They really help alleviate neck tension and beat a wadded-up jacket or plane pillows, which aren't cleaned after each flight. Orthopedic supply stores are a good place to find such items, although some airport and hotel stores sell them as well.

  Another way to save your back and create comfort is to make your own footrest. "They lengthen the lumbar spine and take the pressure off the lower back. It also gets the weight off the hamstring muscles," says Dr. Terri Rock, a family practitioner specializing in travel medicine. If the airline doesn't offer footrests, Rock recommends placing your briefcase or a small suitcase in front of you and propping your feet on top.

  If you have a preexisting back problem, consider wearing a sport belt with a built-in lumbar roll for support. "They not only feel great when you're sitting, but they help you when you carry your bags. It's a wonderful tool to make a five-hour plane ride comfortable—or at least painless," says Dr. Al Loosli, who counsels traveling world-class athletes such as Olympic gold medal winners Kristi Yamaguchi and Matt Biondi. Loosli recommends the support belts as part of a complete rehabilitation program, including back and stomach strengthening exercises. Continue to be careful with your luggage while wearing the belt, especially when placing it overhead, pulling it off the carousel, or loading it into your trunk. Never move heavy luggage after sitting for long periods without "warming up" first by stretching or moving around.

- *Get your back in shape before you leave.* Muscle weakness creates 80 percent of Americans' back pain. "If you're out of shape, you lose the strength necessary to hold good posture," says exercise physiologist Charlie Longdon. "In general, people who are in better shape have fewer back problems." Begin doing some back exercises before the trip, even if you don't presently have back problems. Consult your family physician, a personal trainer, physical therapist, or a source such as the *YMCA Healthy Back Book* (1994) to get a list of good exercises. Make a point of stretching your hamstrings and back before boarding the plane, train, or bus or getting in your car. You might also do a few stretches en route. Sitting shortens your hamstring muscles in the back of your thighs. When you stand up, the shortened hamstrings pull on your pelvis, which throws your back out of line.

And, as we discuss in the next section, don't stay nailed to your chair.

## Get Out of Your Seat

Now that you've found or created that great seat—don't stay in it. Curiously, many air travelers seem to abide by an unwritten rule requiring them to stay seated except for an occasional trip to the lavatory—even on 14-hour flights! Similarly, car travelers often "tough out" marathon drives, only stopping for gas. We want you to break that rule and get out of your car or airplane seat at least every hour or two.

That's because any prolonged sitting, even if you nabbed the best seat on the plane or doctored your car seat for optimal comfort, is stressful for your entire body, not just your back. Your joints become stiff, your muscle tone deteriorates, your reaction time and coordination drop off, your circulation decreases, and less oxygen reaches your organs and muscles. As a result, you feel tired.

Simply walking the length of the plane or train every hour will help to keep your back happy, your muscles supple, and your circulation moving. If you're traveling by car, stop for frequent short "rest-stop walks." If your plane is delayed, and you're not stuck on the runway with the "fasten seat belt" sign on, get off and walk around the airport. John C. Kauphusman, 53, of San Francisco, a retail manager who takes 33 international trips per year, uses the stairway to the upper deck of some 747s as his personal Stairmaster. While the other passengers are sleeping, he climbs the steps several times for some exercise.

Getting out of your seat preferably every hour, but at least every two hours, also prevents a more serious problem called "the economy class syndrome" (referring to the sardine-like seating in coach) or "traveler's thrombosis," a potentially dangerous condition characterized by venous stasis and sometimes by blood clots. Basically, sitting in cramped quarters for an extended period, whether in a car or plane, produces a shift in body fluids, causing blood to "pool" or stagnate in the lower extremities, especially in the veins that return blood to the heart. You feel it when your ankles swell and you can't get your shoes back on.

The combination of blood pooling, pressure on the legs from tight seats, and dehydration set the stage for blood clotting. "Ever since deregulation, airline passengers have been cramped like sardines. This causes circulatory problems in the legs, especially for people who are out of shape," says Dr. Stanley R. Mohler, director of aerospace medicine at Wright State University. Blood clots can form in the legs and pelvis during the long, constricted period of sitting that may dislodge in three hours or three weeks and travel throughout the body, says Dr. Mohler. Trips as short as three or four hours may produce the problem, but it more frequently results from longer trips. While pregnant women, smokers, people with varicose veins or a history of venous disease, and those over 60 or overweight are at greater risk for the condition, doctors around the world have reported cases of traveler's thrombosis even among young, healthy people. Former Vice President Dan Quayle was hospitalized for this after enduring a rigorous travel schedule.

To reduce the threat of blood pooling and clots, doctors suggest that you:

- Walk and stretch every hour.
- Exercise the calf and leg muscles regularly and tighten and release the abdomen and gluteal muscles to help push the blood back to the heart.
- Find a roomy seat with the maximum leg room or upgrade to first class. You can't afford to be in the middle of five seats with neighbors scrunching you!
- Drink water and avoid alcohol to prevent dehydration.
- Wear loose clothing, take your shoes off, and elevate your feet, but don't cross your legs.
- Take regular, deep breaths, and stop smoking (which causes hypoxia and thickening of the blood).

- If you have preexisting venous disease, consider wearing support hose.

Getting out of your seat is the start of keeping your energy level high and avoiding more serious problems. To maximize your fitness in transit, consider punctuating your time in the air or on the road with regular fitness breaks.

# In-Transit Body Moves

What? Exercise in transit? How embarrassing! Perhaps. But, you don't have to do push-ups in the aisle of a 747 to exercise in transit. Lufthansa and Northwest Airlines now show exercise videos at the end of long flights for passengers who want a work out—without leaving their chairs. If you're not lucky enough to have the opportunity to exercise aloft *en masse*, there are some simple isometric and stretching exercises that you can do inconspicuously in transit and still get the benefits of improved circulation and increased energy.

Included here are two seated exercise routines, one for the airplane, the other for the car, and one standing exercise routine which you can do in the airplane's galley or at a rest stop. Each routine combines stretching and isometrics to work your body's major muscle groups— without turning the heads of other passengers or being a bad neighbor. If an entire routine does not work for you, select the exercises that you feel comfortable doing and create a routine of your own. For example, find discreet ways to stretch. You might do what Manhattan-based fitness expert Barbara Pearlman does and deliberately place something in an overhead compartment which you can reach for midflight. The goal is to find a workable way to keep from developing tight muscles and fatigue in transit.

Remember, every bit of exercise helps to improve your fitness level and brings you closer to your fitness goals. So take advantage of the "dead time" in transit to stretch and strengthen your muscles for a few minutes every hour.

## ■ *In-Flight Seated Exercise Routine*

This three-minute in-flight exercise routine can be performed inconspicuously while sitting in your airplane seat. It also can be accomplished on a bus or train. Even the limited movement of this routine will keep your muscles limber and increase circulation. You should repeat this routine at least once every hour.

### 1. Seated Calf Raises

Leaving the balls of your feet on the floor, raise both of your heels, then release. Repeat five times.

### 2. Seated Foot Raises

Leaving the heels of your feet on the floor, lift the balls of your feet, then release. Repeat five times.

### 3. Quadricep Extensions

Straighten your legs as far as the space in front of you will allow. Tighten the muscles in the front of your thigh, hold for 2-3 seconds, then release. Repeat five times.

### 4. Hamstring Isometrics

Press both calves into the front of your seat. Tighten the muscles in the back of your thigh, hold for 2-3 seconds, then release. Repeat five times.

### 5. Abdomen Tighteners

Keeping your lower back firmly pressed against your seat, pull in your abdominal muscles. Hold for 2-3 seconds, then release. Repeat five times.

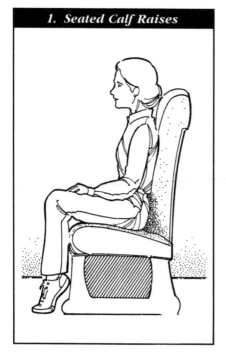
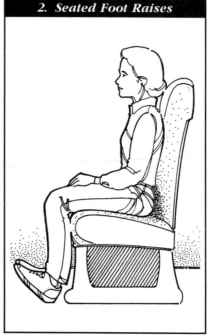

**1. Seated Calf Raises**

**2. Seated Foot Raises**

## 3. Quadricep Extensions

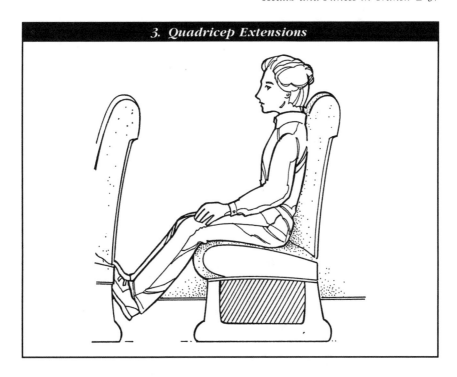

## 4. Hamstring Isometrics

## 5. Abdomen Tighteners

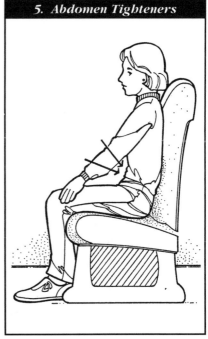

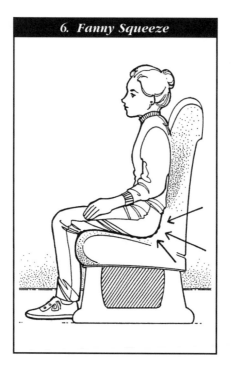

### 6. Fanny Squeeze

Squeeze the buttocks muscles as tight as you can for 2-3 seconds, then release. Repeat five times.

### 7. Seat Walking

Shift the weight from the right to the left side of your fanny, rocking back and forth for 5-10 seconds.

### 8. Pelvic Tilts

Press the small of your back forward, creating a defined arch in the small of your back. Then reverse the movement, pressing your lower back into your seat and pushing your hips forward. Repeat the motion five times.

## 7. Seat Walking

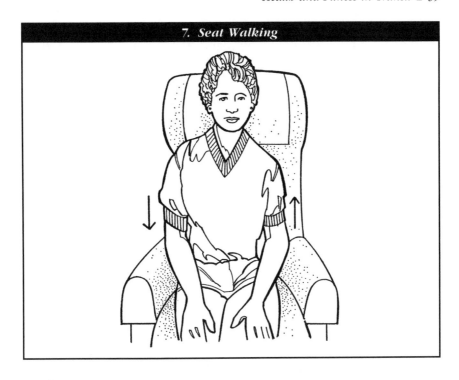

## 8. Pelvic Tilts

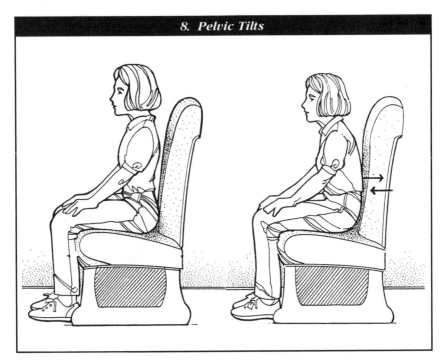

### 9. Back Twist

Holding your armrests, gently twist and stretch your trunk from right to left.

### 10. Lower Back Stretch

Separate your knees, and drop your upper body forward between your knees. Keep your hands on your knees as needed for support.

### 11. Push-Pull Arm Isometrics

Clasping your hands in front of your chest, press your hands firmly together. Hold for 2-3 seconds. Then attempt to pull your hands apart for 2-3 seconds. Repeat the "push-pull" sequence five times.

### 12. Shoulder Shrugs

Lift your shoulders as high as they will go, then release slowly. Repeat five times.

### 13. Shoulder Pull-Backs

Pull your shoulders back, attempting to touch your shoulder blades, then release. Repeat five times.

### 14. Neck Stretches                    *(not illustrated)*

Slowly drop your head to your right shoulder and feel the stretch in

**9. Back Twist**

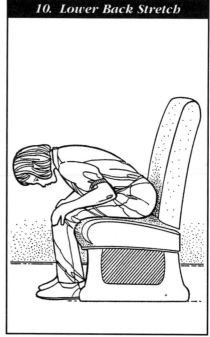

**10. Lower Back Stretch**

## 11. Push-Pull Arm Isometrics

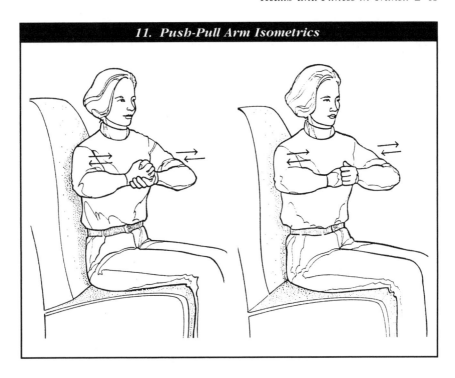

## 12. Shoulder Shrugs

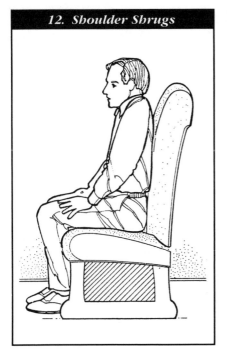

## 13. Shoulder Pull-Backs

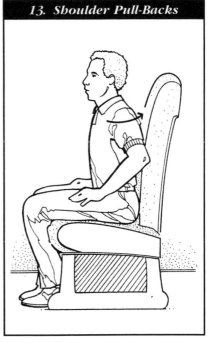

your muscles on the left side of your neck. Hold the stretch for a moment, then lower your chin *toward* your chest to loosen up the muscles in the back of your neck. Finally move your head to your left shoulder. Reverse the sequence until your head is on your right shoulder again.

# ■ *Car Exercise Routine*

Follow this routine only when you are cruising down open stretches of highway no faster than 55 miles an hour. Keep your hands on the wheel at all times. This workout takes about three minutes to complete, and you should perform this once every driving hour.

Start by doing exercises 5-8, 12, and 13 of the In-Flight Seated Exercise Routine. Then add the following exercises:

### 1. Leg Squeezes
Tighten the thigh muscles, hold for 2-3 seconds, then release. Repeat five times.

### 2. Steering Wheel Squeezes
Gripping the wheel with hands at 3:00 and 9:00, squeeze tightly, pressing inward. Hold for 2-3 seconds, then release. Repeat five times.

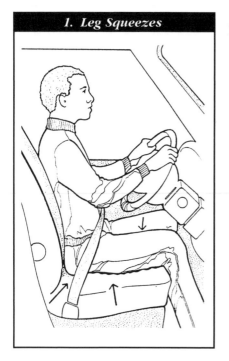

**1. Leg Squeezes**

**2. Steering Wheel Squeezes**

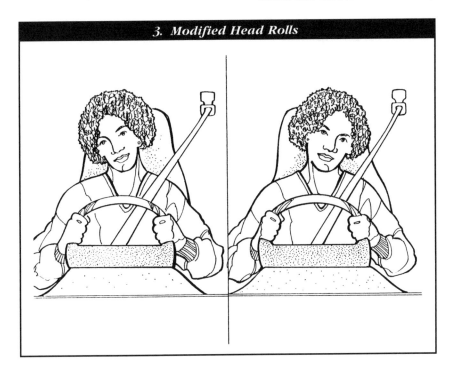

**3. Modified Head Rolls**

### 3. Modified Head Rolls

Tilt your head slightly towards your right shoulder. Bring your head back to center, then tilt it slightly towards your left shoulder.

If you are hooked on car exercising and want to listen to a musical exercise routine while you drive, two audio tapes are available. To obtain *Workout While U Drive* ($9.95), contact Sandra Lotz Fisher at (212) 744-5900. *KarKicks* ($14.95) is available through Events Extraordinaire, (800) 666-2230.

## ■ *Standing Exercise Routine*

Whether you're waiting to catch a flight, confined to an airplane or train, or visiting a rest-stop, this standing exercise routine quickly will restore your energy and loosen tight muscles. This routine takes about two minutes and should be repeated as often as you feel is necessary.

### 1. Calf Raises

Using one hand to balance yourself, raise both heels from the floor, and hold yourself upright on the balls of your feet. Release. Repeat five times. To increase difficulty, raise yourself on one foot at a time.

| 1. Calf Raises | 2. Hamstring Stretch |
| --- | --- |
|  | 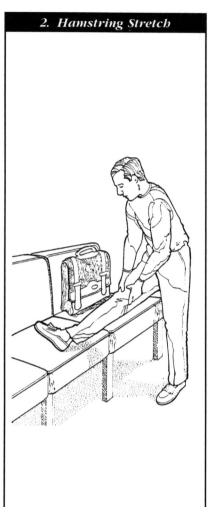 |

## 2. Hamstring Stretch

Using an empty chair, bench, or any object approximately three to four feet high, place the heel of your right foot on the "platform," with your leg extended straight in front of your body. Slowly drop your chest towards your leg, stretching your right hamstring muscle. Keep your back straight and your pelvis in neutral alignment. Hold for several seconds. Repeat with the opposite leg.

### 3. Standing Quadricep Stretch

### 4. Half Squats

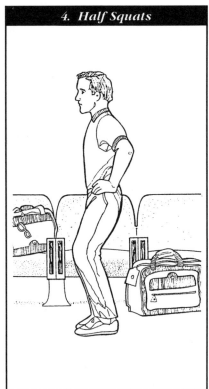

### *3. Standing Quadricep Stretch*

Using your left hand to balance yourself, grab your right ankle with your right hand. Pull up until you feel a stretch in your right front thigh. Reverse and stretch with the opposite leg.

### *4. Half Squats*

Keeping your back straight, bend your knees slightly, and then return to standing. Repeat five times.

### 5. *Standing Back Twist*

Gently twist and stretch your trunk from right to left.

### 6. *Wall Press*

While standing, press both hands into the wall, as if you are trying to move it. Hold for 2-3 seconds. Repeat five times.

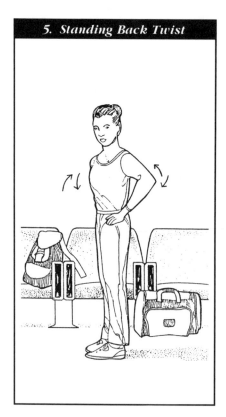

# Layover Fitness Strategies

Airports now seem little better than glorified bus stations, conjuring feelings of both boredom and stress in delayed or stranded passengers. Instead of making a beeline to the airport lounge for relief, use the terminal as an indoor walking track. Simply don your walking shoes, toss your carry-on in a locker, and you're ready to go. The average airport terminal is a half mile long. A whopping 7-1/2 miles of passages connect the four terminals at the Dallas-Ft. Worth airport; that is a challenging walking course for anyone, provided one avoids the conveyor-belt walkways. Mix in a little stretching and you have a great workout.

Woo Daves, 45, of Spring Grove, Virginia, travels at least 225 days a year as a professional bass angler and uses this strategy: "When I have a layover, I try to take advantage of the downtime and I do a lot of walking. Oftentimes my layovers are from 45 minutes to two hours. I try to walk 45 minutes at every airport. I time myself. I give myself a longer time leaving the gate and make myself rush back to catch the flight to keep up the pace."

Make it a point to discover any airport amenity that makes for a healthy fitness diversion. For example, Singapore's Changi Airport has a pool. Or, you can shower and rest after your fitness walk at the Skytel at LAX's Tom Bradley terminal. Another strategy: catch a shuttle to an on-site or adjacent airport hotel for a workout or massage. Many of today's airport hotels are as high-end as their downtown cousins, offering indoor pools, fully-equipped health clubs, racquetball and tennis courts, which are often open to nonguests for a nominal fee. The Hyatt Regency at the Dallas-Ft. Worth airport—a five-minute shuttle ride away from baggage claim—charges nonguests $5 to use its fitness facility, which offers an outdoor heated pool, exercise equipment, and a sauna and steam room. Simply call the general information number at the airport you're traveling through to find out about on-site and nearby amenities. It sure beats sitting in a hard chair, waiting.

# Eating Right in Transit—Four Sensible Strategies

Getting to your destination by plane or car poses a big risk to sensible eating habits and your waistline. At the mercy of airline meals, airport snack-food vendors, and roadside greasy spoons, too many frequent travelers eat whatever is available and wind up overweight and hypertensive. While more airlines are switching to lighter fare, don't let those small portions fool you. You can still rack up more than 900 calories eating a single airline meal with dessert.

Here we present strategies for taking command of your dietary fate in transit. Tips for eating in restaurants and bolstering your travel willpower discussed in Chapter 6 apply to the in-transit portion of your journey as well.

## 1. Order a Special Meal

You can avoid the mass-produced, dietary landmines your neighbors are eating aloft by ordering a special meal in advance. It's as simple as calling the airline—there's no extra cost to you. Airlines require from 3- to 36-hours notice. Some frequent fliers place a standing order with their carrier so they are automatically served their meal of choice, or they simply request the meal when they book their flight.

Special meals are usually fresher, prepared the day before or the day of departure, and better tasting, too. The number of choices—including Hindu, Muslim, kosher, heart-healthy, low fat, low cholesterol, low sodium, vegetarian, gluten-free, lactose-free, diabetic—keeps growing. Lufthansa even serves a raw vegetarian meal. Qantas offers the longest menu—29 special meals! Some airlines, like TWA, provide the specific nutritional content of their meals to interested passengers.

The cold fruit and seafood platters rate high for taste among finicky diners because they don't suffer the ravages of reheating. Says traveling chef Martin Yan: "My friends and I order a special seafood platter. That's probably the most delicious way, because when it's prepared cold and served cold, you don't have any deterioration of the quality."

## 2. Never Travel Hungry

Don't start your six-hour drive or board the plane hungry. You will just end up making poor dietary decisions. "Honor your hunger; it's important to keep somewhat fed no matter what. Never go for more than five hours without food," says Evelyn Tribole, M.S., R.D., author of *Eating on the Run* (1992).

By waiting too long to eat, Tribole warns, travelers fall victim to the "I don't care, feed me" syndrome. "Your biological hunger gets so strong, it becomes primal," she says. "Travelers then are more apt to reach for whatever is available, including Häagen-Dazs or other goodies."

Never assume there will be meal service on your flight—call ahead. Many airlines have eliminated meals on flights under 500 miles or 80 minutes and are replacing real meals with snacks on longer flights. "You never know what will happen," says Sandra Lotz Fisher, a New York-based exercise physiologist who counsels business people on how to maintain their health while they travel. "I have sat on the runway for three hours at a time thinking I was going to get a meal that never arrived."

To avoid in-transit hunger attacks, pack healthy snacks or buy them at the airport or roadside grocery store. Many flight attendants skip airplane meals entirely. Other travelers like Kristi Reimers, of Omaha, who travels every month as a nutritionist for the Center for Human

Nutrition, eats a combination of airline food and snacks she brings on board. On shorter trips, eat your meal before you leave. That will increase your willpower to decline unhealthy food.

## 3. Eat Lightly

Fighter pilots at Edwards Air Force Base are told to make more than half their meal be vegetables, fruits and grains, and to avoid gas-inducing foods before their trips. Experts say you'll feel better, too, if you eat lightly en route. It's even better if you begin to eat lightly the day before leaving. Focus on cereals, breads, vegetables, fruit, and low-fat dairy products, supplemented by fish, poultry, legumes, and small amounts of eggs and cheese for protein. "You don't want to squander energy digesting big meals when your body is under stress while traveling," says Dr. Bagshaw of the Physis Prevention Center. "The key is to eat lightly."

If you must grapple with regular airplane fare, Evelyn Tribole offers these tips for keeping it light:

- Don't eat the nuts; they can be from 60 percent to 93 percent fat calories.
- Cut down on fat by reducing your intake of margarine and salad dressing, peeling the skin from chicken, and skipping dessert.
- At breakfast, skip the high-cholesterol, fatty eggs and sausage; opt instead for cold cereal and fruit.
- If a business meal awaits you when you arrive, skip the plane meal. Don't view the airplane meal as a snack, she says.
- Drink lots of water! "Many people gravitate towards food when they are really dehydrated," says Tribole. "They eat more than they should."

## 4. Eat for the Right Reason

Are you eating for entertainment? To feel comforted? Because you're bored? To compensate for the rigors of the road? If you're suddenly craving a slice of Pizza Hut's pepperoni pizza at the airport in Sydney, Australia, ask yourself why. You may discover that you really aren't hungry; you just want a reminder from home or a reward for surviving the trip. For frequent travelers, that split-second increase in awareness, over time, can mean the difference between racking up the pounds and keeping slim and fit. If boredom drives you to binge, airport layovers can spell diet disaster, Tribole says. She recommends planned

# TRAVEL FITNESS TIPS:
# TOP 10 IN-TRANSIT STRESS BUSTERS

1. **Avoid ups, downs, peak travel times, and busy airports.**
   Take nonstop flights—versus direct, which may include stopovers—whenever possible to avoid layovers and decrease
   your chances of delayed or canceled flights. Try to avoid
   travel on Mondays and Fridays and rush hours of 7 a.m. to
   9 a.m. and 4 p.m. to 7 p.m. Consider midweek travel as an
   option. Another stressor to avoid: congested airports. Many
   savvy fliers won't touch down in crowded hub airports such
   as Hartsfield International in Atlanta, opting for satellite airports or alternative routes instead. If you're spending too
   much time waiting in airports, join an airline membership
   club. For an annual fee—in the $100 plus range, varying by
   airline—you'll gain access to the club lounge, where you
   can sip fruit juice, watch television, read a complimentary
   newspaper or magazine, or tackle a business project. You'll
   also be able to avoid the long public check-in lines, select
   seats, and make further reservations with the airline representative present in most club lounges.

2. **Schedule extra time to get there.** If a meeting is scheduled
   for 10 a.m., don't catch a flight arriving at 9 a.m., or head
   out in your car with not a minute to spare. Give yourself
   plenty of time to catch your plane and make your meeting
   to avoid unnecessary stress.

3. **Catch a pretrip workout.** If you're leaving early in the
   morning, exercise the night before. If you're leaving in the
   afternoon, exercise in the morning. It will relax you, and
   you may not mind sitting in the car or plane as much with
   a little muscle fatigue. Remember, the better shape you're
   in before you leave, the better you'll feel in transit.

4. **Adopt a healthy in-transit attitude.** How you feel about
   getting there depends, like most things in life, on your attitude. Frequent traveler Randy Petersen adopts a Zen-like
   attitude to travel: "Canceled flights and missed meetings don't

bother me anymore because there's not much point in worrying about what you can't control." Be creative when things go wrong and look at the downtime as an opportunity. For example, if you have an unexpected layover, use the extra time to contemplate one of your life's goals and brainstorm ways to achieve it. Many travelers find that scheduling a post-trip reward improves their in-transit attitude. After a long flight, Steve Campbell heads for the shiatsu clinic near his office in Tokyo for a massage.

5. **Practice deep breathing.** When stressed, one of our first responses is to hold our breath and tighten our chests. If you're in a plane, constricted breathing just adds to the mild hypoxia you might already be experiencing. When you're en route, make it a point to take in four to five deep breaths every hour.

6. **Pack variety into your trip.** View your time in the air or on the road as your personal private time. Don't spend the whole time working on the plane or listening to sales tapes in your car. Listen to audio books or relaxation, how-to, or music tapes, or play with a hand-held electronic game. Use the time to think or meditate. Some of the best ideas were born cruising down an interstate.

7. **Create a personal travel mantra.** Carry in your head a phrase or two that affirms positive qualities in you, stated in the present tense, to help you cope with in-transit stress. For example, the phrase, "I am where I'm supposed to be," might help you relax when a situation develops that's out of your control. When you feel stress, repeat the phrase a few times in your head. It really can help you relax.

8. **Don't drive more than six to eight hours a day**. The stress from long drives can interfere with your driving and job performance once you arrive. Experts suggest not driving more than 400 miles a day and never driving after an emotional upset. One study indicated one of five drivers killed in automobile accidents had experienced emotional distress within six hours before the accident.

9. **Take a short nap.** Pull your car over to a rest-stop or recline your seat on the plane, and take a short nap. Just don't let your snooze exceed 30 to 40 minutes, which could disrupt

> your sleep-wake cycle and make it hard to get to sleep at night.
>
> 10. **Indulge yourself in an on-board massage.** If you happen to be an upper class (first class) passenger on one of Virgin Atlantic Airway's flights from London to Japan or the United States, have your tired, achy muscles worked on by the free, on-board masseuse! Or sit in an in-flight automatic massage chair. Japan Airlines offers its "sky massage" service—a specially equipped chair offering 15-minutes of pounding, rolling, or shiatsu massage—on flights between Tokyo and New York and on the Tokyo-London route.

distractions: bringing along a good book or music, catching an airport workout, or catching up on work.

# Combating Four Common In-Transit Perils

Sometimes, despite our best efforts, we feel ill or uncomfortable in transit. Let's look at four of the most common travel ills and how to remedy them.

## Earaches

Changing cabin pressure can cause ear discomfort, even pain. That's because it creates a difference in pressure between the middle ear and outer ear. As the plane ascends, air pressure in the cabin decreases, causing excess pressure in the middle ear. Air then is pushed outward through the eustachian tube until pressure is equalized. This happens naturally, or by swallowing, says Dr. Blair Simmons, professor of medicine and a specialist in ear, nose, and throat problems at Stanford Medical School. Descent, however, causes the most problems for ears, says Dr. Simmons. On descent, pressure increases in the environment, causing under-pressure in the ears. To equalize the pressure, air must reenter the middle ear through the eustachian tube. Swallowing, yawning, or chewing gum will usually accomplish the task because those actions work the muscles that open the eustachian tube. But if you have a cold or are sleeping, the negative pressure can suck in the eustachian tube so that it cannot open. This can cause significant pain and temporary (one or two days) hearing loss, Dr. Simmons says.

While you shouldn't fly with a cold or allergies, many business travelers don't have the luxury of postponing a trip. Dr. Simmons offers these tips for keeping your ears happy at 30,000 feet:

- *Learn how to open the eustachian tube.* Swallow, chew gum, or yawn as soon as you feel the plane descending. If that fails, try the Valsalva Maneuver, named after a 17th-century Italian. Take a deep breath, pushing out the chest, but keep the air in. Hold your nose, and then blow into your closed nose and swallow. You should experience a clicking sensation in your ears and relief from ear discomfort.

- *If you have a stuffy nose, cold, or allergies, use a decongestant.* Spray decongestant in each nostril a half hour before descent. But don't overuse such products. Your nose will actually become more congested after the decongestant wears off, which encourages repeated use.

- *Don't sleep during descent.* You won't be able to tend to your ears if you're sound asleep.

- *Don't drink alcohol.* Alcohol causes your mucous and eustachian tube to swell, exacerbating "airplane ears."

## Noise stress

You may have noticed some crew members wearing noise-proof earphones back in the galley. There's a good reason: The loud hissing, whirring sounds produced by jet engines, especially in economy class, can cause temporary hearing loss, says Dr. Simmons. "People often complain that their ears feel stuffy after a flight. This is not always due to pressure problems. Often noise in the cabin is sufficient to cause it," he says. The best way to avoid stuffy ears: sit in front of the engines and wear ear plugs.

## Altitude sickness

If during a long flight you are short of breath, nauseated, lightheaded, or headachy, you may be feeling the stress of insufficient oxygen. Many travelers shrug off their bad feelings. But people who have respiratory problems, who smoke, or are ill or on certain medications may feel real discomfort and should consult with a physician before flying. Airlines carry oxygen tanks for such severe cases. For the otherwise healthy traveler experiencing mild hypoxia, experts recommend resting, eating lightly, and drinking water. You might also try "pressure-breathing," a technique to increase atmospheric pressure in the lungs and oxygen content in your bloodstream. Jack Cummings, author of *The Business Travel Survival Guide* (1991), describes the technique he learned in the Air Force this way: Take a deep breath and hold it for two seconds. Then begin releasing, slowly, about 20 percent of the air through your mouth. With 80 percent of the air still in your lungs, close your mouth tightly. Continue trying to push the air out through your closed mouth, but not too hard. Hold for about two seconds, then exhale. Take one or two normal breaths, then begin again. Do no more than 10 pressure breaths, with alternating normal breaths. Cummings says you may feel lightheaded for a short time, but should get relief from your symptoms.

## Motion sickness

Maybe the plane just hit a pocket of clear-air turbulence, or your car just maneuvered another curve on a windy road. Suddenly, you're headachy and dizzy and breaking a cold sweat. You feel uneasy and nauseated. Wherever it strikes, motion sickness affects most travelers at some time in their lives.

Many scientists believe the syndrome is rooted in the brain's response to conflicting sensory information sent by the eyes and ears. When your car winds around a bend in the road, your inner ears detect motion. But if you're reading in the back seat, as far as your eyes are concerned, you're not moving at all. Confused by the sensory mismatch, the brain releases a surge of stress hormones, which can produce nausea. "The body says, 'O.K., we can't take this anymore; we have to do something'," says Dr. Kenneth L. Koch, a specialist in motion sickness at Pennsylvania State University's Milton S. Hershey Medical Center. That something is "reverse peristalsis," or vomiting. Another theory focuses on the inner ear's balance center: Excessive motion in the inner ear's balance center can lead to nausea.

Here are some suggestions to avoid the syndrome:

- Change locations to experience less motion. Move from the back seat of the car to the front. If you're in the cabin of a plane, move to an aisle seat directly above the wing, the stillest spot on any plane.

- Get some fresh air as soon as you start to feel ill. Stop the car and take a rest break. On a plane, turn the overhead air vent on, and sit as far away as possible from the smoking section.

- Don't overeat, smoke, or drink alcohol. A light, starchy snack such as crackers can help.

- Look at the motion your body is experiencing. Don't read, focus on anything close by, or close your eyes. Many car travelers benefit from looking at the horizon, at something far away, or at the road ahead. Keep in mind that you're better able to focus on distant points from the front seat of a car.

- Keep your body, especially your head, still.

- Don't worry—this will just flood your stomach with more stress hormones. Stay busy or focus on more pleasant thoughts. Loosen your clothing, recline your seat, or listen to calming music on the headset. Take several deep breaths, as you concentrate on relaxing your muscles.

- Various drugs and remedies are available, including a skin patch worn behind the ear containing scopolamine, but some people experience side effects similar to motion sickness from medications. Some travelers swear by less traditional remedies such as acupressure wrist bands that stimulate the "anti-nausea" Neiguan acupuncture point on the inside forearm, just above the wrist. Others take ginger, a home remedy for gastric upset, in tea or capsule form, to calm their topsy-turvy stomachs.

Take heart, most travelers eventually adapt to motion sickness.

## Surviving the Red-Eye Special

To maximize productivity and to save money, some business people work all day, fly all night, rush to an early morning meeting, and fly home in the late afternoon—never taking a hotel room or missing a day of work in transit. These fast-track travelers pay a high price, says Dr. Charles F. Ehret, co-author of *Overcoming Jet Lag* (1983), who maintains that red-eye flights "wreak havoc" on the body.

"It is a bad idea. In the end, these people are going to lose several days of their lives because of the resulting mental dysfunction. Businessmen out to make a buck are going to make a lot of mistakes instead of a profit," he said in an interview with the *Los Angeles Times*.

The best advice: Never take a red-eye flight unless you can sleep on the plane. While some red-eye travelers maintain they sleep from takeoff to landing, most don't get the quality of sleep they need.

Veterans of nighttime flights have many strategies for creative cabin sleeping. They wear eye shades, earplugs, and comfortable clothes. Nothing beats a reclining seat in first class, but those in coach have some nifty options, too. After grabbing a pillow and blanket, some fliers head for the back of the plane and secure an empty row, lift the arm rests, and stretch out. They immediately feign sleep to dissuade other passengers from bothering them. The most coveted prize: an unoccupied row of five seats. Failing at that, some will even find a place on the floor to "go horizontal."

If you're forced to sleep sitting up, an inflatable pillow collar lets you relax while it supports your head in a near-upright position. Avoid sitting near the lavatory; the foot traffic might keep you up. Alas, the future might hold the answer to in-flight sleeping problems: Airbus will soon introduce sleeping quarters in the cargo section of its A-340 aircraft.

# The Fitness in Transit Checklist

Here's a round-up of the key points for staying fit in transit.

❏ Take nonstop flights.

❏ Avoid hub airports and peak travel times.

❏ Allow extra time to get there.

❏ Exercise before you go.

❏ Pack your own bottled water.

❏ Drink at least one 8-ounce glass of water per hour in flight.

❏ In flight, avoid alcohol and salty foods.

❏ Dress comfortably.

❏ Book a bulkhead or emergency exit row aisle seat.

❏ Use an inflatable lumbar roll or support belt for your back.

❏ Get out of your seat every hour or two.

❏ Perform discreet exercises while in transit.

❏ Walk during an airport layover.

❏ Order a special meal.

❏ Never travel hungry.

❏ Eat lightly in transit.

❏ Avoid red-eye specials.

# Coping With
# Jet Lag

**J**et lag affects nearly all long-distance fliers. Henry Kissinger noted in *The White House Years* that he had trouble during the Vietnam peace negotiations because of jet lag. Greg Louganis hit his head on the 10-meter diving board at the Moscow Olympic trials and attributed it to a long flight. Studies show that NFL players, pilots, traveling business people, and even race horses suffer malaise and reduced performance after crossing many time zones traveling east or west.

The sometimes serious, always annoying, symptoms of jet lag start the minute you get off the plane after a transmeridian flight. Your wristwatch is on a new time, but your body thinks it's still back home. You may feel tired, headachy, or disoriented. You may find yourself wanting to sleep or eat at odd times. Your eight-minute mile becomes a 10-minute mile. Normally alert, you now can't perform well at meetings and find it difficult to concentrate for any length of time. While the symptoms of jet lag are diverse, affecting each person differently, one thing is for certain: No one is entirely immune to jet lag. But there's much a time-zoned-out traveler can do to speed the adjustment process. Begin by gaining an understanding of the causes for this often-misunderstood travelers' complaint. Take the following quiz to **Test Your Jet Lag I.Q.**

## Test Your Jet Lag I.Q.

Read each statement below and mark true or false in the corresponding blank space.

1. The speed at which most commercial aircraft travel contributes to jet lag. _____

2. It's easier on your body to travel eastward than westward. _____

3. Jet lag affects young people more than people middle-aged or older. _____

4. One of the key causes of jet lag is fatigue caused by travel. _____

5. There's very little you can do to combat jet lag; you just need to "wait it out." _____

6. Becoming dehydrated in flight and breathing stale cabin air induce jet lag. _____

7. Jet lag is exclusively a problem of difficulty in sleeping. _____

8. Studies suggest that introverts adjust more readily to jet lag. _____

9. If you want to adjust to a new time zone, the most important thing is to make sure to sleep whenever you feel tired. _____

10. A traveler can succumb to jet lag on long north-south flights even if there's no change in time zones. _____

None of the above statements concerning jet lag is true. In the pages that follow, we will debunk many common beliefs about jet lag and give you scientifically backed strategies for coping.

# What's Jet Lag?

An internal clock out of sync with a new time zone is at the root of a cluster of problems—from fatigue, insomnia, and poor performance to irritability, digestive upsets, and headaches—called *circadian dysrhythmia*, or jet lag.

Your biological clock, tucked away in two tiny portals in the brain called the suprachiasmatic nuclei, acts along with the pineal gland (also located deep in your brain) as an internal timer governing virtually every biochemical process of the body. The clock runs the body's principal rhythms on cycles of about 24 hours, called circadian, from the Latin *circa* meaning "about" and *dies* or "day," and sets itself to the light-dark cycle where you live. If you were isolated in a cave, unable to sense day or night, your natural rhythms would "free run" at slightly longer intervals, creating a 25-hour day.

Under a consistent light-dark cycle, your internal rhythms synchronize with each other and with the daily environmental rhythms of sunrise and sunset. This delicate balance is disrupted when you're suddenly transported by jet to a new time zone and a different light-dark cycle. For example, if you depart from New York for Europe at 7 p.m. and arrive at 5 a.m. local time (midnight New York time), your day-night cycle would be inverted, throwing your body rhythms off kilter. While sleep-inducing hormones course through your body, you're supposed to dash to a morning business meeting and perform at your peak. This temporary state of desynchronization between your internal and external worlds is jet lag. The accompanying table (p. 62) shows the many internal cycles disrupted by jet lag.

Ultimately your reluctant body rhythms will adapt to the new environment. But if left to their own devices, they won't do it overnight. Typically it takes one day or more to recover for each time zone crossed. That means a New York to Europe excursion could leave you out of sync for a week.

# Common Misconceptions

Many people associate jet lag with flying at high speeds or altitudes. Or they believe eating bad airplane food, breathing stale cabin air, becoming dehydrated in the arid plane environment, or sitting in a cramped seat will subject them to jet lag's torments. They think the stress of leaving home, waiting in long ticket lines, or lugging suitcases through the terminal makes them vulnerable to jet lag. Many believe

## Cycles Disturbed by Jet Lag

| Rapid ("Ultradian") | Daily ("Circadian") | Weekly/monthly ("Infradian") |
|---|---|---|
| Brain waves | Digestion | Reproduction |
| Cell division | * Bowel movements | * Ovulation |
| Eyesight | * Urinary output | * Menstruation |
| * Blinking | * Hunger pains | * Hormone levels |
| Heart | Eyesight | |
| * Heartbeat | Hair growth | |
| * Pulse rate | Heart | |
| Lungs | * Blood pressure | |
| * Breathing | * Blood clotting | |
| Swallowing | Mental ability | |
| | * Alertness | |
| | * Visual acuity | |
| | * Cognitive function | |
| | Metabolism | |
| | Physical ability | |
| | * Physical prowess | |
| | * Energy level | |
| | * Sense of pain | |
| | Reproduction | |
| | * Hormone levels | |
| | Sense of time | |
| | Sleep/wake | |
| | Temperature | |

*Note.* Reprinted by permission of The Putnam Berkley Group from *Overcoming Jet Lag* by Charles F. Ehret and Lynn Waller Scanlon. Copyright © 1983 by Charles F. Ehret and Lynn Waller Scanlon.

it's "all in their head," or that if only they were physically tougher, they could avoid it. However, jet lag is not caused by any of the perils of transit discussed in Chapter 2, although those factors can certainly make you feel lousy. It's not simply travel fatigue. And you can't avoid it by simply changing your mental attitude, although this may motivate you to work harder to overcome jet lag's effects.

Jet lag is exclusively a problem of changing time frames and occurs only after long east-west flights. While you might feel less than optimal after a flight from New York to Panama, you won't suffer jet lag because you'll still be on your home time. What's more, you won't suffer jet lag crossing time zones by car, train, bus, or ship because you'll be traveling slow enough to adjust as you go.

# Symptoms of Jet Lag: What to Look For

Because virtually every biochemical process and bodily function is meshed to your 24-hour clock, the internal dislocation caused by changing time zones can manifest itself in a variety of irksome symptoms, which add up to altered performance and impaired functioning. Difficulty sleeping is one of the most common complaints. But even if you sleep well at your destination, you probably still will feel tired and out-of-sorts from jet lag because so many of your other bodily functions are out of sync. The following table describes some of the jet lag symptoms you may experience after arriving at your new locale.

| *Early and Late Jet Lag Symptoms* | |
| --- | --- |
| **Early symptoms** | **Late symptoms** |
| Confusion | Acute fatigue |
| Disorientation | Constipation or diarrhea |
| Fatigue | Decreased muscle tone |
| Off-schedule bowel and urinary movements | Disrupted phases of body rhythms and functions |
| Onset of memory loss | Headache |
| Reduced mental acuity | Impaired night vision |
| Reduced physical ability | Insomnia |
| Upset appetite | Interference with prescription drugs |
| | Lack of sexual interest |
| | Limited peripheral vision |
| | Loss of appetite |
| | Reduced motor coordination and reflex time |
| | Reduced physical work capacity |
| | Slowed response time to visual stimulation |

*Note.* Reprinted by permission of The Putnam Berkley Group from *Overcoming Jet Lag* by Charles F. Ehret and Lynn Waller Scanlon. Copyright © 1983 by Charles F. Ehret and Lynn Waller Scanlon.

The length of time necessary to resynchronize your circadian rhythms varies, as more fully discussed below, according to many factors, including direction of travel, length of flight, and individual differences. As a general rule, without intervention it will take a day or more to adjust for each time zone crossed. The two resynchronization tables shown below and on the next page spell out the time necessary for specific body functions to adjust, depending on the direction of travel.

Recent research suggests that it may take your rhythms even longer than anyone suspected to settle into a comfortable pattern. Scientists at the New Jersey Medical Center recently documented a second drop in psychomotor and cognitive tasks, at least in monkeys, occurring 10 to 14 days after the initial onset of jet lag, a phenomenon dubbed "jet bounce." In a study on monkeys, jet lag symptoms were induced and then subsided as anticipated. What surprised scientists was that about 10 to 14 days after getting used to their new time zone, the monkeys had a second drop in performance that was significant.

"It was large enough to be comparable to what you might expect with a legal dose of alcohol," says Dr. Walter N. Tapp, professor of neurobiology at the New Jersey Medical Center and Veterans Administration Hospital. After receiving more than a hundred letters from jet travelers complaining of recurring malaise, mental impairment, and other jet lag symptoms after an initial period of recovery, Dr. Tapp

## Typical Number of Days Until Resynchronization After Time Zone Changes—Eastbound Flights

| | Time zone changes (in hours) | | | | | |
| | 2 | 4 | 6 | 8 | 10 | 12 |
| --- | --- | --- | --- | --- | --- | --- |
| Adrenaline | 2 | 4 | 6 | 8 | 8-10 | 8-10 |
| Body temperature | 3 | 6 | 9 | 12 | 12 | 12+ |
| Bowel movements | 3 | 6-7 | 9-10 | 12 | 12 | 12+ |
| Heart rate | 2 | 4 | 6 | 8 | 8-10 | 8-10 |
| Performance (psychomotor) | 3 | 6-7 | 9-10 | 12 | 12 | 12+ |
| Reaction time (vigilance) | 1-2 | 3-4 | 5 | 6-7 | 8 | 8 |
| Sleep pattern | 1 | 3-4 | 4-5 | 6-7 | 8-9 | 8-9 |

*Note.* Reprinted by permission of The Putnam Berkley Group from *Overcoming Jet Lag* by Charles F. Ehret and Lynn Waller Scanlon. Copyright © 1983 by Charles F. Ehret and Lynn Waller Scanlon.

## Typical Number of Days Until Resynchronization After Time Zone Changes—Westbound Flights

| | Time zone changes (in hours) | | | | | |
|---|---|---|---|---|---|---|
| | **2** | **4** | **6** | **8** | **10** | **12** |
| Adrenaline | 1-2 | 2-3 | 4 | 5-6 | 6-7 | 8-10 |
| Body temperature | 2 | 4 | 6 | 8 | 10 | 12+ |
| Bowel movements | 2-3 | 4-5 | 7 | 9 | 11 | 12+ |
| Heart rate | 1-2 | 2-3 | 4 | 5-6 | 6-7 | 8-10 |
| Performance (psychomotor) | 2 | 4 | 6 | 8 | 10 | 12+ |
| Reaction time (vigilance) | 1 | 1-2 | 2-3 | 3 | 4 | 5-8 |
| Sleep pattern | 1 | 2 | 3-4 | 4-5 | 6-7 | 8-9 |

*Note.* Reprinted by permission of The Putnam Berkley Group from *Overcoming Jet Lag* by Charles F. Ehret and Lynn Waller Scanlon. Copyright © 1983 by Charles F. Ehret and Lynn Waller Scanlon.

suspects that jet bounce occurs in people as well. More research is needed to fully understand how jet bounce affects human travelers, he says.

# Assessing Your Risk

How do you know when you will fall prey to jet lag and its debilitating effects? Paying attention to your body as you travel extensively is probably the best way to anticipate how you will respond on a given trip. People vary dramatically in how they cope with changes in environmental time. Some sensitive souls require a week to adjust to or from daylight saving time, while others can shuttle across several times zones without a hitch. This makes it critical for you to learn and adjust for your own body's response. Pay attention to these factors that may play a role in how you'll cope:

- Number of time zones crossed
- Direction of travel
- Your age
- Personality type
- Your rhythms

- Whether you're a night owl or a lark
- Your travel habits

## Number of Time Zones Crossed

Most of our biological clocks can make an immediate adjustment to one hour earlier or one hour later than our home times. "When you need to enter a time zone two or three hours different from your own, that's where the difficulty comes in," says Dr. Alex Adu Clerk, director of the Stanford University Sleep Disorders Clinic. Expect that your jet lag symptoms will be worse and will last longer the more time zones you cross, he says. Use an international time zones map (found in most day planners) to count the number of time zone changes on your next flight.

## Direction of Travel

As we mentioned, you won't suffer jet lag on any north-south flight in the same time zone. Although you may feel exhausted from the flight, your biological clock still meshes perfectly with your environment. East-west or west-east flights, however, pose a real challenge, and traveling west-east will be tougher than east-west. Traveling east produces more disturbance to the circadian rhythms, causing symptoms that last longer and are more severe. That's because flying eastward shortens the day, forcing you to squeeze your naturally longer circadian cycle (25 hours) into even less time. The body finds it easier to stay up late than to get up early.

For some travelers, like flight attendant Linda Rocha, 45, of Roseville, California, traveling east is truly grueling. Rocha, while working on American Airline's Chicago-to-Europe route, typically commuted on an early morning flight from California to Chicago and then departed on a working flight to Europe in the late afternoon.

"I felt terrible. I couldn't do it. Going east doesn't work for me. When I arrived it would be daylight, and I was exhausted. What's the sense of being in Paris if you're asleep the whole time?" she says.

Conversely, if you're flying westward, you're adding to your day in harmony with your natural rhythms. Readjustment from a westbound trip, consequently, is from 30 to 50 percent faster than from an eastbound one.

## Your Age

If you're middle-aged or older, jet lag may affect you more severely. As we age, our biological clocks don't recover as well to shifts in environmental time. Sleep disruption caused by jet lag lasts longer in older people. Studies by NASA show that older pilots have a tougher time obtaining sound sleep than their younger counterparts after rapid, multiple time zone shifts. In one study, pilots over 50 lost 3.5 times more sleep at night than the 20- to 30-year-olds after crossing time zones. Beginning in middle age, our sleep tends to become less restful because of changes in the underlying circadian rhythms. Experts say that drastic time zone changes are especially taxing on the elderly because they're starting their journey with an already dysfunctional body clock.

## Personality Type

Are you outgoing, impulsive, uninhibited? Do you prefer group activities to time spent alone? If so, you just might handle jet lag better than an introverted travel companion. There's some evidence to suggest that individuals who score high for extroversion on personality tests adjust more rapidly to time zone changes. This may be because extroverted travelers are more apt to be active and immerse themselves in the new social milieu, helping to speed their adjustment. Many scientists, however, believe the issue is more complicated than simple personality types, which may reflect complex biochemical differences.

## Your Rhythms

Particular characteristics of an individual's circadian rhythms may predict his or her adjustment rate to new environmental time. Russian researchers have measured circadian rhythm stability. Depending on the stability of their rhythms, individuals are either "inert," "intermediate," or "labile." Inert people find it tough to adapt to time zone changes because they have more rigid circadian rhythms. Labile types adjust readily because their rhythms are open to change. Intermediate people fall somewhere between the two extremes.

## Night Owl/Lark

In general, early risers, or "larks," who exhibit more rigidity in their rhythms, seem to have a harder time coping with jet lag than their night owl counterparts with more labile circadian systems. However, larks will fare better heading east because getting up earlier comes naturally to them; night owls will do better heading west. People who sleep less also seem to adjust to jet lag faster than those who routinely sleep eight or more hours a night.

## *Your Travel Habits*

Do you find time to exercise outdoors no matter what your travel schedule? Do you arrive rested, or are you sleep-deprived from last-minute packing and work commitments? Do you eat lightly, or do you use travel as an excuse to overindulge in food and alcohol? The habits you adopt on your trip will play a key role in how you cope with jet lag. As we discuss below, your inner body clock is reset more quickly if you spend time outdoors exercising soon after you arrive. Jet lag's effects also will be minimized if you arrive rested, eat lightly, and avoid alcohol.

# What's Your Response?

From our many interviews with frequent travelers, we've identified the following five jet lag coping styles.

1. *Denial.* This traveler just won't accept that jet lag affects him. Asked about jet lag, this type responds: "I don't have it." "I don't think about it." "I just do my job, and learn to live with it." This traveler sometimes turns to chemical stimulants and artificial sleep aids to mask his symptoms of jet lag. This style is seen more commonly in men.

2. *Toughing it out.* A traveler with this coping style will jet across seven time zones on a red-eye flight and, on arrival, hustle through a jam-packed business day. The quintessential "Type-A" personality, he or she won't allow a minute to adjust, relying instead on adrenaline and sheer willpower to perform. Pushed to the limit, these "tough" travelers often crash and burn when they get home.

3. *Resignation.* "Nothing works, I can't avoid it" is a common refrain among this group of travelers. They struggle through their trips like resigned zombies, admitting to the full impact of jet lag, but doing little to overcome it. They don't believe there's anything they can do to change their travel fate.

4. *Refusal to travel.* Some people just stop traveling. They switch jobs, even careers, to avoid long-distance travel and the jet lag it produces. These types even decline leisure travel that will take them across time zones and only travel when absolutely necessary.

5. *Positive change.* These folks are motivated to reduce the malaise of jet lag and experiment with ways to do it. They pay attention

to their bodies and note what does and doesn't work for them. They build into their travel plans strategies to cope with jet lag and feel and perform better as a result. For example, Melissa Price, 25, of New York, used to tough out jet lag until it started to affect her job as a producer of TV-magazine inserts. Now, with some simple changes, she's coping with jet lag. "When I first started traveling, I couldn't sleep right the first four or five nights in a new area. Now, I mentally and physically prepare for the trip. I always fly in a full day early to get oriented and relaxed. That way, when I start work I'm effective. It works out so much better; I just feel better."

Of the five coping styles, denial, toughing it out, and resignation will only keep you on course for feeling lousy after long east or west flights. While refusing to travel will avoid jet lag, we think an earthbound career and missed adventure is too high a price to pay to keep your circadian rhythms in sync. In the remainder of this chapter we'll offer simple tips, culled from the latest scientific research, to help you adopt a strategy of positive change to beat jet lag on your next trip.

## When Should You Do as the Romans Do?

The first step for time zone changers is to know when to "do as the Romans do"—adopting the new local time and adjusting your biological clock—and when to stay on your home time. Obviously, if you fly the Concord from Washington, DC to Europe for a key meeting and return to your own bed that night, you don't need to worry about shifting your biological clock because you won't be away long enough. Experts say that for shorter trips of one week or less, you probably should keep on your home schedule of sleep and waking. Otherwise, you'll just have made the adjustment to local time, and it will be time to switch to the time back home.

"Just stay on your old time and schedule appointments for when you're alert in the old time zone," says Dr. Peter Hauri, director of the Mayo Clinic Insomnia Research and Treatment Program and coauthor of *No More Sleepless Nights* (1991). Dr. Hauri, when traveling from the Midwest to the West Coast for short trips, wakes up early by West Coast standards, about 5 a.m., and goes to bed early, about 9 p.m., to stay on Midwest time.

For short trips across two or three time zones, consider splitting the difference between your time and local time. Live "somewhere

---

### TRAVEL FITNESS TIPS: A PILL FOR JET LAG

On the horizon for bedraggled travelers within the next two years or so is an FDA-approved anti-jet lag pill that helps reset the body's clock. The pill contains melatonin, dubbed the "Dracula hormone" because it's produced by the pineal gland only at night. Melatonin is a powerful internal time-giver, sending information to every organ in the body as to time of day. The hormone gives cues to the biological clock, independent of light and with the opposite effects. Light has an alerting influence; melatonin induces sleep. By administering the pill at different times of the day, Dr. Lewy and others have successfully shifted the biological clocks of adults and "tricked" the body into thinking it's light or dark. Melatonin taken before or during the trip has been shown to eliminate jet lag by resetting the body's clock. The combination of melatonin and light therapy may prove the best defense against jet lag, says Dr. Lewy.

---

in the middle of the change," advises Dr. Bagshaw of the Physis Prevention Center. For example, if you're flying from Los Angeles to New York, think about going to bed 1 to 1-1/2 hours earlier (not three hours) and getting up 1 to 1-1/2 hours earlier. That way, you can still schedule a morning business meeting, and the split time keeps you closer to the one hour adjustment which most of us can make.

Science can't now tell us how far to travel or how many time zones to cross before it seems sensible for a traveler to adopt local time. It really comes down to what works for you. Most experts agree, however, that it's probably best to adjust to local time for trips lasting a week or longer and taking you across two or more time zones. The key is to begin to adjust your sleep-wake cycle before you leave home.

"For those longer trips, it's important to make adjustments in your clock before you go so when you arrive at your new destination you're within the one hour adjustment range," says Dr. Clerk. Take two or three days before your trip to begin the adjustment, even if you won't be able to complete it. To use the Los Angeles to New

York example, try going to bed one hour earlier for the two nights preceding the trip. That way, when you arrive in New York, you'll only have to make a manageable one-hour time change. Of course, the pretrip adjustment process will be tougher traveling east because it requires you to go to bed earlier, squeezing your already compressed biological clock into an even shorter day.

If last-minute scheduling or other conflicts make it impossible to adjust before leaving, experts agree that on longer trips the traveler should switch immediately to the new time zone. Start as soon as you board the plane. Change your watch to the new time to help make the psychological adjustment. If it's daylight at your destination and you're on a night flight, turn on the overhead light and keep active— read a book, listen to music, write a letter, move around the plane. Try to stay awake for the duration of your flight. If it's nighttime at your destination, keep the window shade drawn and try to relax or sleep. When you arrive, immerse yourself fully into the local pace of life. Stop calculating in your head what time it is at home. Eat when the locals eat. Stay active during daylight. No matter how much you want to sleep, wait until it's bedtime in the new place. Then, get up, the same time each day, at a reasonable local time. Late wake-ups and social isolation will only impede your adjustment.

# The Light Stuff

To help them beat jet lag, pilots for Japan Airlines bask in bright light in a special room at San Francisco International Airport before flights. Shuttle astronauts receive "light therapy" before missions requiring nighttime work to help them sleep during the day and be alert at night. The Grand Hyatt in Taipei, Taiwan, the Rembrandt Hotel in London and the Tudor Hotel in New York offer jet-lag rooms where guests can use a jet-lag visor that emits bright light. The airlines may someday offer "light-class service," exposing passengers to light before they reach their destination.

Why? Because bright light is the single most potent external factor that can reset the biological clock and speed up the body's adjustment to a new time zone. Your circadian rhythms reset themselves primarily in response to light.

Light acts as a powerful cue—a time giver—telling your clock where you are and what schedule to keep, thereby persuading your circadian rhythms to synchronize with each other and with the new environment. After entering the retina, light shoots right to those 10,000 cells comprising your biological clock, alerting the brain to wake up. "That alertness increases for a while and then wanes, ending in drowsiness and sleep," says Dr. Clerk.

Recently, Charles A. Czeisler, an eminent researcher in the field of circadian rhythms at Brigham and Women's Hospital in Boston, and his colleagues demonstrated the powerful effect of light on the biological clock. Exposing subjects to bright light, they discovered that light applied before the "circadian midnight," around 4 to 5 a.m. when body temperature is lowest, turns the clock back. Application of light after this time pushes it ahead. "Properly timed exposure to light can shift us the equivalent of any time zone or reset the biological clock by up to 12 hours in just two to three days," said Dr. Czeisler in an interview with the *New York Times.* "With just a single light exposure of three to four hours around breakfast time, we can get you half way to Europe."

While you may not want to visit a sleep lab in the wee hours of the morning to be doused with light, there are some simple steps you can take to use natural light when you arrive at your destination to speed your adjustment process to the new time zone.

Begin by booking a daytime arrival. Memorize this simple travel rule:

Fly east early; fly west late.

If you are heading east, get an early start so there's plenty of daylight when you arrive. For example, if you fly from the East Coast to Europe early in the morning, you won't be frazzled from taking a red-eye. Although you'll lose five or more hours by skipping time zones, you'll still arrive during the early evening and can immediately begin to reset your clock by getting outdoors. If you instead opt to fly at night, you'll lose a night's rest, which would only impair your ability to get in sync. When heading home, leave later. There's no reason to lose any sleep catching an early morning flight heading from Europe to the United States, because by heading westward you'll be gaining daylight with each time zone crossed.

When you arrive at your destination, "drag your tired body outside and stay out in the bright light," says Dr. Hauri. Studies have shown that travelers who spend several hours outside in natural light after arrival recover from jet lag at least twice as quickly as those who do not. The last thing you should do is nap in the shadows of your hotel room. Being holed up in a hotel conference room won't do the trick either. That's because the intensity of the light required to reset the body's internal clock must be about five times brighter than indoor light. You don't have to sunbathe. Being outdoors during the day under virtually any conditions, even sitting in the shade or strolling along the Seine on a rainy or cloudy day, will give you sufficiently bright light to reset your clock.

The size and direction of the shift depend on when light is applied in the circadian cycle. The human clock subscribes to a pattern of organization called a "phase response curve," which can be advanced or delayed depending on the timing of light exposure. Dr. Al Lewy, a psychiatrist at the Oregon Health Sciences University in Portland and a pioneer in light therapy, has developed practical tips for seeking and avoiding light at certain times of day, depending on the direction of travel and the number of time zones crossed, to phase-shift your biological clock and beat jet lag. It's equally important to *avoid* light at specified times as it is to seek it, because you don't want to create an unwanted phase shift. "If you get light at the wrong time, you could send your clock around the world in the opposite direction than you want to. Then you're really going to have a very difficult time adjusting because you're going through so many more time zones that way," says Dr. Lewy.

In general, if you're traveling east, try to get at least one hour of light early in the morning after arriving to advance your clock to help you get to bed earlier and get up earlier. The table below shows the optimal times to seek and avoid light on eastward trips.

If you're traveling west, seek at least one hour of sunlight in the late afternoon, which will help to delay your clock to help you stay

## Timing of Light Exposure for Eastbound Flights

| Time difference from departure point | Stay indoors: (local time) | Be outdoors: (local time) |
|---|---|---|
| 2 hours | — | 6 a.m.–8 a.m. |
| 4 hours | — | 6 a.m.–10 a.m. |
| 6 hours | — | 6 a.m.–noon |
| 8 hours | 6 a.m.–8 a.m. | 8 a.m.–2 p.m. |
| 10 hours | 6 a.m.–10 a.m. | 10 a.m.–4 p.m. |
| 12 hours | noon–6 p.m. | 6 a.m.–noon |

From *Beat Jet Lag*, by Kathleen Mayes, p. 46. Copyright 1991 by Kathleen Mayes. Adapted with permission.

*Note.* This table assumes a 6 a.m. sunrise and 6 p.m. sunset.

## Timing of Light Exposure for Westbound Flights

| Time difference from departure point | Stay indoors: (local time) | Be outdoors: (local time) |
|:---:|:---:|:---:|
| 2 hours | — | 4 p.m.–6 p.m. |
| 4 hours | — | 2 p.m.–6 p.m. |
| 6 hours | — | noon–6 p.m. |
| 8 hours | 4 p.m.–6 p.m. | 10 a.m.–4 p.m. |
| 10 hours | 2 p.m.–6 p.m. | 8 a.m.–2 p.m. |
| 12 hours | noon–6 p.m. | 6 a.m.–noon |

From *Beat Jet Lag*, by Kathleen Mayes, p. 46. Copyright 1991 by Kathleen Mayes. Adapted with permission.

*Note.* This table assumes a 6 a.m. sunrise and a 6 p.m. sunset.

alert longer and get up later. The table above shows the best times to seek and avoid light on westward trips.

Of course, if you're traveling to Norway in the winter, there probably won't be enough available outdoor light to shift your internal rhythms. Just do the best you can under the circumstances. It doesn't take a lot of work. Just build into your schedule, as nature permits, when you'll get your dose of photons. Keep spending time outdoors during the optimal times when there is available light. Do whatever it takes— dine alfresco, work outdoors, walk to your appointments, meditate or read a newspaper on a park bench, jog or stroll in a local park. If you can't remember when to be outdoors, simply "go outside when you feel like sleeping," advises Dr. Hauri. You can beat jet lag in two or three days, but not if you are cloistered in an office or conference room.

For those who want precision, Dr. Martin Moore-Ede of the Institute of Circadian Physiology has created a computer program that, given a traveler's itinerary, provides detailed advice on when to seek light and when to avoid it. The service is offered through Circadian Travel Technologies, 7315 Wisconsin Avenue, Suite 1300-W, Bethesda, MD 20814-3202, (301) 961-8559.

# The Exercise/Activity Connection

If you jog, walk, play tennis, or engage in any other type of exercise when you arrive, you just might take the punch out of jet lag. Evidence suggests that exercise helps to rapidly readjust your internal circadian rhythms to a new time zone. Researchers at the University of Toronto showed that a three-hour round of exercise helped hamsters beat a severe case of jet lag. The exercising rodents adjusted to jet lag in a day and a half; their couch potato counterparts took eight days to adjust. While it's a big stretch from hamsters to humans, most experts agree that a daily program of exercise will help you beat jet lag.

There's plenty of anecdotal evidence that lends support to the exercise connection. For example, U.S. infantrymen transported to Europe who immediately trained outdoors to become combat ready, adjusted to the new time zone within about two days. Their commanding officers, who were inactive and stayed indoors, still suffered from jet lag two weeks after arrival. Many of the travelers we interviewed use exercise religiously to cope with jet lag. For example, Jim Topinka, who travels regularly from San Francisco to Washington, DC, exercises as soon as he reaches his destination to beat jet lag. "I'll immediately find a swimming pool and go swimming. My travel agent knows that I won't stay in a hotel unless it has a lap pool. I just feel so much better. It's that simple," he says.

Outdoor exercise offers additional benefits to help you adjust when you arrive. "It gets you moving with the social cues of your new environment, it gets you fatigued so you can sleep better, and it gets you out in the sun," says Dr. Joe Tupin, a jet lag expert and professor of psychiatry at the University of California-Davis. Ideally, if you're traveling east, exercise outside in the morning; if you're traveling west, exercise outside in the late afternoon or early evening. That way, you'll expose yourself to bright light at the optimal times and gain the many benefits of exercise.

## Six Ways to Prevent Your Jet Lag From Getting Worse

Keep the following tips in mind the next time you're scheduled for a long transmeridian flight. If you neglect even one of them, your ability to tackle jet lag will be impaired.

### 1. Give Yourself a Day or Two to Adjust After a Long Flight

Barbara Wambach, 33, vice president of destinations merchandising for Duty Free in San Francisco, travels internationally six months of the year. Her grueling travel schedule often puts her in the position

## TRAVEL FITNESS TIPS: EMERGENCY COUNTERMEASURES TO STAY ALERT UNTIL YOUR BODY CATCHES UP

Let's say you've adjusted your sleep pattern before departing, embraced local customs, doused yourself with photons, and run every morning since you've arrived and your body still hasn't adjusted to the new time zone. You've stumbled along so far in your less-than-optimal state, but now you're called on to make a decision affecting people's lives, speak at an important seminar, pitch a key client, or compete in an athletic event. What can you do? These strategies won't reset your body clock, but they will provide acute relief to the fatigue and mental fuzziness caused by jet lag.

- **Take a "NASA Nap."** NASA has conducted extensive research on ways to improve flight crew performance and alertness after rapid, multiple time zone shifts. In one study, pilots who took a 40- to 45-minute nap had improved performance and physiological alertness compared to pilots who did not nap. If you have a high-performance activity ahead, take a nap for not longer than 45 minutes. Longer naps take you into the deep stages of sleep, making you feel groggy when you wake. Be careful; too many naps will only put off your adjustment to a new time zone.

- **Use caffeine strategically.** Some evidence links caffeine to improved athletic performance, and NASA has administered it to pilots on long-haul flights with positive results. "If you're heading into a circadian rhythm slump, drink coffee 15 to 30 minutes in advance of when you need to be alert," says Dr. Mark Rosekind, a research scientist at NASA's Ames Research Center. But don't overindulge—eight cups of coffee will dehydrate you and give you a case of the coffee jitters. Quit drinking coffee four to five hours before bedtime so you can get to sleep.

- **Stay physically active.** "The earliest sleep deprivation studies showed that the best way to keep someone awake is through physical activity. Take frequent breaks, get up, walk around, talk to people, participate in meetings," advises Dr. Rosekind. Consider taking a refreshing swim or a brisk walk before an important event.

- **Schedule your most critical activities at a time when your energy level would be at its peak at home.** For example, if you're a Midwesterner conducting business in London, you might schedule business meetings in the late afternoon for the first few days since that would be morning time at home. Consider creating an escape hatch for botched decisions. For example, insert a 24-hour rescission clause in any important document, or insist that any big deals be subject to confirmation at a later date.

- **Eat for energy/calm.** A number of authors have offered diet programs to beat jet lag. Dr. Charles F. Ehret's book, *Overcoming Jet Lag* (1983), which proposes a feast/famine diet to prepare the body for a circadian phase shift, has received much anecdotal support, but also some skepticism from leading scientists. The idea that alteration in diet can rapidly shift circadian rhythms is based mainly on experiments with animals. Limited data on humans suggests that our rhythms are less susceptible to diet changes. But your choice of food may help you get to sleep or stay awake. In *Beat Jet Lag* (1991), Kathleen Mayes recommends eating foods high in protein and low in fat, such as poached eggs, low-fat cottage cheese, low-fat yogurt, or grilled fish, early in the day to boost physical energy and mental alertness. Eat foods high in carbohydrates, such as breads, pastas, fruits, and vegetables, later in the day to induce sleep.

- **Visualize alertness.** There's evidence that visualization improves sport and academic performance. Why not gain a psychological edge on jet lag by imagining yourself alert and effective before a big event? While your mind alone can't reset your body clock, it can help you cope.

of flying all night to immediately begin a hectic business day in a foreign city. Too frequently, she doesn't schedule an "adjustment day" before undertaking serious work. "I've had occasions where I'll fly all night, arrive in Paris at 7 a.m., and go straight to work," she says. Like so many other pressed business travelers, Wambach suffers as a result.

Because transmeridian travel almost always produces some impairment in judgment and performance, it just isn't smart to dive into important business deals or engage in a hectic social schedule too soon after landing. Unless you're disciplined enough to gradually switch to the time zone of your destination before you go, it's best to allow an adjustment period when you arrive. Dr. Loosli, who counsels the U.S. swim team, requires that when traveling to Europe for important meets, swimmers arrive a full two weeks ahead to ensure peak performance. At a minimum, allow yourself one day of rest after crossing four to six time zones, and at least two days of rest after crossing seven or more time zones. You might schedule stopovers on long-haul flights. For example, if you're traveling to Australia from the West Coast, spend a night in Hawaii. If your work schedule just won't allow for "rest days" during the week, consider arriving at your destination the weekend before your work week. At the very least, schedule your least demanding activities for your first day or two in town and save your more challenging work for later in the trip, after you've had a chance to recover.

## 2. Travel Rested

"I just don't have time to get enough sleep before leaving." That's a common lament among travelers. Many board the plane exhausted; others arrive sleep-starved after a red-eye special. The result is a terrible case of jet lag as you lose even more sleep at your destination because of a dislocated sleep-wake cycle.

Poor planning and poor scheduling are the two biggest culprits causing pretrip sleep loss. To avoid arriving sleep-deprived, don't work late the night before your trip, putting out fires and clearing paperwork. Instead, start preparing for your trip several days in advance. Anticipate your workload, and don't leave travel arrangements and packing until the last minute. Most importantly, get plenty of sleep the week before you leave. To beat jet lag, you must arrive rested.

## 3. Avoid Alcohol and Sleep Aids

Many folks rely on a nightcap or sleeping pill to get to sleep in a new time zone. The danger is that alcohol and many other sleep aids taken by travelers disturb circadian rhythms, cause other negative effects, and pose the potential for abuse, says Dr. Tapp. "There are some people who try to manipulate their system, but the problem with alcohol and a number of these compounds is that they have other effects. They can eliminate your ability to think and concentrate, and destroy your memory," he says. One hapless traveler who took Halcion to sleep made a lost luggage claim in Frankfurt, only to be told she had just made one. A few hours later she found herself in Heidelberg, with no recollection of how she got there. Another international traveler who took Halcion en route was spotted during a layover in Los Angeles reading the same page of the *Los Angeles Times* for three hours. He reboarded the plane for a four-hour flight to Chicago and, as the plane made its descent at O'Hare International Airport, asked his travel companion, "You mean we're in Los Angeles already?" Experts advise using alcohol and sleeping pills sparingly, if at all.

## 4. Stay Hydrated

It's essential to avoid dehydration for your circadian rhythms to have a chance of adjusting to the new time zone. "There's a good argument that dehydration negatively affects the circadian cycle—and it's certainly going to affect your performance and the way you feel. That's a potential double whammy," says Dr. Tapp. So if you want to overcome jet lag, drink lots of water.

## 5. Eat Sensibly

Overeating—a temptation on any trip—will only compound the lethargy and fatigue caused by jet lag. Heavy, rich meals burden your digestive system when it's already dysfunctional from jet lag. The travelers who cope best with jet lag really watch what they eat on the road and make an effort to eat lightly. John Kauphusman was ready to throw in the towel on his career in retail management because of the grueling international travel it entailed. "When I first started traveling, I wasn't doing anything to cope and I felt terrible. I thought, I'm never going to be able to do this with any regularity." John overhauled his on-the-road habits, including his approach to food. He now opts for salads and orders light Asian dishes when in the Orient, instead of fatty, pseudo-American fare. The approach worked: He now successfully manages 33 international trips a year.

## 6. Go Easy on Yourself

Too many folks underestimate the amount of stress involved as they traverse multiple time zones, hurtling headlong into a disorienting array of environmental changes—from time of day to temperature, food, and customs. Your body is bombarded with stressors, even on the most pleasurable vacation, and deserves a break. Avoid over-scheduling your days and follow Seattle-based flight attendant Colleen O'Neal's advice: Never push yourself too much when you travel.

# The Jet Lag Checklist

Here are the basics for coping with jet lag.

❏ Assess your risk.

❏ Decide whether to shift your clock.

❏ Adjust your sleep pattern before you go.

❏ Book a daytime arrival.

❏ Arrive rested.

❏ Allow a day or two to adjust.

❏ For the first day or two, expose yourself to daylight at the appropriate time.

❏ Exercise shortly after arrival, preferably outdoors.

❏ Do as the Romans do.

❏ Avoid alcohol and sleep aids.

❏ Stay hydrated.

❏ Eat sensibly.

❏ Go easy on yourself.

# Getting to Sleep

**Y**ou're exhausted from the journey, but you can't sleep. You toss and turn in the sagging hotel bed. Your mind races, your muscles tense. Your stomach remembers too well the extra cocktail you drank on the plane. You glance at the clock: It's 3 a.m. Your wake-up call is set for 6 a.m., and a key meeting is less than five hours away. You *must* sleep. You struggle against the sheets, anxious and angry, for another hour. Finally, you drift into a fitful, twilight sleep until the alarm sounds.

You're experiencing traveler's insomnia—that frustrating inability either to get to sleep or to stay asleep that strikes every traveler at one time or another. Travelers say it's one of the most vexing challenges to fitness and performance they face while away from home. In fact, probably nothing hampers one's physical and emotional balance on the road more than poor sleep. It darkens your mood, zaps your energy, dulls your mental alertness, and squelches your creativity.

If you're already sleeping poorly, it will only worsen on the road. Even if you sleep well at home, you will face challenges to good sleep while away. "Business travelers have so much working against them, it's almost expected that in new places they won't sleep well," says Dr. Peter Hauri. The good news: you can take simple, practical steps to increase your chances of sound sleep on the road. The first step to relief from traveler's insomnia is understanding the mechanics of normal sleep and how travel disrupts it.

## The Basics of Normal Sleep

What is this thing called sleep? Actually, there are two kinds of sleep: non-REM, also called deep, normal, slow-wave, or orthodox sleep; and REM, the more exciting variety. REM stands for "rapid eye movement," a light stage of sleep when your eyes move about quickly and dreaming occurs. (During REM sleep, you're more likely to be awakened by unfamiliar sounds in your hotel room). Scientists believe that REM sleep restores mental functioning, while non-REM recharges the body.

During the night, the two sleep types alternate as the sleeper journeys through four to six cycles of sleep. Each cycle lasts about 90 minutes and consists of four deepening stages of non-REM sleep, ending in a blast of REM. Just after retiring, you enter stage one, a transition period, just the other side of wakefulness. A fit sleeper quickly—usually within five minutes—reaches stage two, still a light sleep, but deeper than stage one. About 30 minutes after sleep onset, a good sleeper descends into stages three and four, the really deep stages of sleep, where he or she remains for as long as 40 minutes. The sleeper then invariably rolls over from one side to the other, moves back to stage two sleep, and begins dreaming. (We all dream—every sleep-filled night). After dreaming ends, the cycle begins again. As the night wears on, non-REM sleep lightens while dreaming increases, from about five minutes at the end of the first cycle to 30 minutes or more after the fourth cycle.

"The important thing is not what stages of sleep you're having, but the total amount and quality of sleep you get. It is important that you not have much stage one sleep and that your sleep be continuous, not fragmented with awakenings. That's why most sleep clinicians are more concerned that you sleep well than whether the sleep is this or that particular stage," writes Dr. Hauri in *No More Sleepless Nights.*

How much sleep is enough for the road-weary business traveler? Experts agree that there simply is no normal amount of sleep. Sleep needs vary dramatically among people: some need as little as three hours to feel rested, while others require ten. Travel, exercise, and stress can increase the need for sleep. The key is to know the amount of sleep that really works for you, not the amount you can get by on as a sleep-starved zombie. If you don't know how much you need, track the number of hours you sleep on your next vacation of a week or longer (leave the alarm clock at home), and take the average. Dr. Wilse Webb, a psychologist at the University of Florida and author of *Sleep: The Gentle Tyrant* (1991), has a simple test for telling whether you are getting enough sleep: If you feel rested when you wake up and do not feel tired until bedtime, you are getting sufficient sleep.

# What Causes Traveler's Insomnia?

For the jet-hopping business traveler, impaired sleep is a hazard of the road. Frequent travelers report that their sleep is more disturbed, often peppered with many awakenings, and they do not get enough of it. Simply put, you suffer from traveler's insomnia if you cannot easily fall asleep, or if you cannot stay asleep, when you are away from home. Insomnia is classified as transient (one to three nights), short-term (three nights to three weeks), or chronic (more than three weeks). Traveler's insomnia typically is transient or short term, but may become chronic if travel is constant and the cause of the sleep problem remains unidentified and untreated.

Here we will focus on the three primary causes of insomnia on the road: your disrupted biological clock, poor sleep hygiene, and stress.

## *The Disrupted Biological Clock*

An internal clock out of sync with a new time zone is a key cause of lost sleep, one of many symptoms commonly referred to as jet lag, discussed in Chapter 3. Because your biological clock tells you when it's time to sleep, any disruption in the timing of your normal sleep-wake cycle can lead to insomnia. Jet lag can make it difficult to fall asleep and to stay asleep. Even if you can sleep, the quality of your sleep may be poor, making you feel tired the next day. For frequent business travelers, trouble with the clock causing sleep problems is as common as lost luggage. "The main thing causing sleep disturbances in travelers is the disruption to the biological clock. The key is the change in environmental time; the body needs time to adjust itself," says Dr. Alex Adu Clerk.

Luckily for the time-zoned-out business traveler, you don't have to suffer insomnia waiting for your biological clock to synchronize with local time. Follow the jet lag coping strategies discussed in Chapter 3 to reset your sleep-wake cycle if jet lag is causing your sleep difficulties.

## Poor On-the-Road Sleep Hygiene

While traveling, do you conduct business right up to bed time? Do you find yourself not going to the gym because you don't have the time? Do you drink nightcaps to help you sleep? While in bed, does your mind often buzz with worries about tomorrow's business? Do you stay in bed even when you can't sleep?

If you answered "yes" to one or more of these questions, you may have what sleep doctors call poor "sleep hygiene." All too many business travelers develop bad habits on the road which interfere with good sleep. They pay the price in sluggishness and slow thinking the next day.

"A lot of people hurt themselves with sleep because they feel that being on the road demands war pay. So war pay comes in the form of an extra cocktail or eating more than they should," say Dr. Bagshaw.

Sleep doctors agree that simple changes in behavior—such as cutting out alcohol and caffeine—can help people beat insomnia. In fact, studies show that behavioral methods can be more effective than sleeping pills in fighting poor sleep.

If you're a bleary-eyed, sleep-deprived traveler, take the time to improve sleep habits. Adopting some of the "good sleep" tips discussed below could alleviate your traveler's insomnia.

## Stressed Out and Unable to Sleep

*"You're always thrown a curve ball on the road; something always goes wrong."*

—J. Randall McDermott, 30, of Boca Raton, Florida, who travels
    150,000 miles a year as president of Voxx Communications

*"The time pressures of my job are enormous. It's complicated even more on the road. I have to deal with the normal pressures of my work and with the aggravation of being on the road."*
—Judge Gary Schmidt, 44, of California, Missouri, who travels 100 days a year

*"It's the hardest thing traveling. I'm all alone, facing new people and places, always dealing with the unknown. Many nights, I just can't sleep right."*
—New York-based traveler Melissa Price

Do you hear yourself in these words? Then stress may be preventing you from catching your ZZZs on the road.

Insomnia is a 24-hour disorder: What happens during the day affects how you sleep at night. Unfortunately for many, business travel means round-the-clock stress. Rushing to catch the plane, being sandwiched for hours in a metal tube hurtling across the sky, or grappling with ground transportation in a new city can all conspire to rob you of sleep.

"There's a strong psychological basis to many, if not most, cases of insomnia, and stress plays a major role," said Allan Luks, executive director of the Institute for the Advancement of Health in New York, in an interview with *Parents* magazine. Studies suggest that people who feel in control of their lives sleep better than those who do not. The harried business traveler who feels at the mercy of events outside of his or her control risks losing sleep. Experts agree, moreover, that increased mental arousal caused by the stress of travel disrupts the delicate mechanism of sleep. If you're a stressed-out traveler, learning some of the simple stress management techniques addressed in Chapter 7 may help you get to sleep.

## How High Is Your Travel Sleep Debt?

If you're traveling regularly, sleep loss can be serious business. In an interview with *Parade* magazine, H. Craig Heller, a professor of biology at Stanford University who studies sleep, compares sleep to a bank account. "You have to keep some minimum balance. If you keep on making withdrawals without making deposits, you run up a deficit. Then the pressure builds, biologically, to 'deposit' some sleep."

Your brain, acting the ever-vigilant bookkeeper, may demand payback of the accumulating debt when you're not expecting it. "People can go from feeling wide awake to falling asleep in five seconds. If you are behind the wheel of a car, you're dead," says Dr. William C.

Dement, a leading sleep scientist and author of *The Sleepwatchers* (1992). In fact, sleepiness is implicated in more automobile accidents than alcohol. What's more, sleep loss played a significant role in the Exxon Valdez oil tanker spill in Alaska, the 1986 Space Shuttle Challenger disaster, and the Chernobyl and Three Mile Island nuclear accidents.

While the consequences of sleep loss may not be as catastrophic as Chernobyl for the business traveler, they should be taken seriously. Think of all the times your job demands a clear, alert head for making critical decisions, speaking at meetings, poring through documents, and other tasks. Your creative and critical judgment skills suffer most from lost sleep. "It can make the difference between performing adequately and performing optimally," says James Walsh, head of the Sleep Disorders Center at Deaconess Hospital in St. Louis.

Missing a night or two of sleep on the road will not hurt your body, and the adrenaline rush from travel often counteracts the short-term effects of not sleeping. But if you're on the road every month missing sleep, you may be racking up a sizable sleep debt. In one NASA study of long-haul pilots, 85 percent had accumulated a sleep debt by the fourth day of a trip.

Sleep doctors say that we are remarkably inaccurate in judging our level of sleepiness and unknowingly may be carrying a large sleep debt. Here are some telltale signs that you may have traveled into the red:

- You cannot wake up without an alarm clock.
- You sleep more on the weekends, or when you get home from a trip.
- At home, you fall asleep within five minutes of putting your head on the pillow.
- You nod off on airplanes, during lectures, in front of the TV, at the movies, or while talking with your spouse (without intending to).
- You feel drowsy off and on throughout the day.
- You feel short-tempered, irritable, disorganized, and/or anxious.
- Colleagues at work have mentioned that your performance has fallen off.

Recognizing the seriousness of sleepiness and the signs of your own accumulating travel sleep debt is the first step to relief. Fortunately, one good night's sleep (waking without an alarm clock) is usually enough to regain 90 percent of mental alertness, and another good night's sleep retrieves the other 10 percent, say sleep experts. Reducing any sizeable debt, of course, takes longer. But you don't have to make up for all the sleep you missed. Writes Dr. Hauri in *No More Sleepless Nights*: "If you have been totally deprived of sleep for about ten days, you will probably sleep for 14 or 18 hours per day for about three days and then go back to your normal schedule."

# Habits to Sleep By

Good sleep hygiene is more important than ever when you are on the road. If you want to travel and stay fit over the long haul, incorporate some of the simple good sleep principles outlined below on your next trip.

You might consider keeping a travel sleep log to see which suggestions work for you, says Dr. Hauri. Simply record in a journal how you sleep each night on the road and what you did the day before. You will discover over time which of these good sleep habits are essential to combat your own brand of traveler's insomnia.

## Create a Good Sleep Pattern at Home and Stick to It

To sleep fit on the road, you first need to be sleeping well at home. "You don't want your sleep-wake cycle to be arrhythmic before you leave," says Dr. Clerk. "This would make your ability to sleep on the road even tougher."

There are two keys to creating a good sleep pattern—a regular bedtime and wake-up time—says Dr. Clerk. The one that should never be sacrificed is your wake-up time. Get up at about the same time every day, including weekends, no matter how poorly you slept the night before. (If you sleep in after a bad night, you will begin to displace your natural rhythm). In fact, the experts agree that the more serious the insomnia, the more a regular wake-up time is needed. This sort of regularity keeps your circadian sleep-wake cycle running smoothly—and will give you a healthy start on the road.

## Eliminate or Reduce Your Sleep Debt Before You Go

If you're already running on empty, get some extra sleep before you go. According to one Stanford study, of all the factors associated with jet lag (and its characteristic insomnia), the primary one is pretrip sleep loss. "Before a trip, everyone is staying up late, packing, worrying, getting things in order. People are sleep-deprived before they start," says Dr. Mark Rosekind, who studies ways to prevent or reduce the effects of sleep loss and circadian disruption on flight crew performance. "Two or three nights before going on a trip, people should get more sleep. If you're already sleep-deprived when you start on the road, it's only going to get worse."

## Control Your New Environment

Whether it's a forced-air heater that won't turn off, light peering in from behind the curtains, unfamiliar noises, or a mattress that couldn't support you even if you lost that extra 20 pounds, the typical hotel room can be downright hostile to good sleep. If you want to sleep well, you need to take control. The frequent travelers we spoke with shared the following 12 tips for creating an environment conducive to sleep:

- Ask for a king-size bed, no matter what.
- Sleep diagonally to avoid the "body tracks" of an over-worn mattress; or ask the concierge for a board to place under a soft mattress to protect your back and help you sleep.
- Immediately check to see if the temperature control is working in your room. If it is not working, change rooms.
- Keep your room on the cool side; it helps you sleep.
- Never take a room by an elevator, facing a busy street or airport, or near an indoor pool. The extra foot traffic and noise will keep you awake.
- Wear ear plugs (and set two alarms to make sure you wake up).
- Always put out the "do not disturb" sign.
- Take along a travel humidifier: it creates "white noise" to block out unfamiliar sounds and prevents excessive dryness.
- Wear an eye mask to block unwanted light.
- Bring your own pillow.
- Bring reminders from home, such as a photo or your favorite pajamas. They will make you feel that you are in a familiar place and will help you sleep.
- If you feel unsafe, leave the bathroom light on.

## Hide the Hotel Clock

"Before going to bed, the absolutely number-one thing is to hide the clock. Make absolutely certain that you can't see the clock in the hotel room," says Dr. Hauri. "Knowing that it's 3 a.m. and you have to get up at 6 a.m. guarantees that you won't sleep for the remaining three hours." So arrange for your wake-up call or set the alarm, then hide the clock.

## Make Yourself Drowsy Before You Sleep

Many business travelers work like mad right up to bedtime and then wonder why they can't get to sleep. You should begin to wind down from demanding activities at least one to two hours before bedtime. Put an end to late-night meetings. Replace them with a warm bath, relaxing music, light reading, or other low-key activities. Go to sleep only when you are feeling drowsy.

## Take Your Rituals on the Road

Most of us have bedtime rituals which we observe every night. We read a book, eat a light snack, brush our teeth, arrange the pillows—all acts which help our transition into sleep. "Whatever ritual you do at home, do the same thing in your hotel room, maybe even in a more pronounced way," says Dr. Hauri. "For example, if you take a shower before bed at home, take a really long, hot shower in the hotel room."

## Use Well-Timed Exercise to Help You Sleep

Exercise is probably the best sleep medicine available. Studies show that the fit sleep better than the flaccid. Exercise helps so much because it tires the body, releases stress, and helps to reset your circadian rhythm after crossing time zones. It also combats insomnia in another way—by raising your body temperature. Our body temperature rhythmically increases during the day and decreases during the night. In insomniacs the rhythm is suppressed: their temperature does not increase as much during the day (because they are less active and alert) and does not decrease as much at night (causing light, fragmented sleep). Regular exercise in the late afternoon or early evening, ideally five or six hours before bed, avoids this problem because it raises your body temperature, which then drops off as you are getting ready for bed. Decreasing body temperature triggers the onset of sleep and promotes a deep sleep. Timing is everything: if you exercise too early in the day, you will not benefit from the cool down; if you exercise within three hours before bed, you may be too stimulated to sleep.

Try to engage in vigorous exercise (anything that raises your pulse) for 20 minutes at least three or four times a week in the late afternoon or early evening, about five to six hours before going to bed. Any exercise is fine as long as it raises your body temperature about two degrees Fahrenheit, advises Dr. Hauri. If exercise cannot be squeezed into your business agenda, Dr. Hauri suggests sitting in the hotel's Jacuzzi or taking a hot bath for 20 minutes in the late afternoon or early evening. The rise in body temperature should create the same sleep-inducing effects as exercise.

## Sleep on a Light Stomach

The status of your stomach at bedtime affects how well you'll sleep. Avoid heavy meals late at night—a stomach busy digesting food will keep you awake. Schedule dinner four or five hours before bedtime, and keep it light. It's best to have your biggest meal in the morning with a lighter lunch and an even lighter dinner. Don't scrimp too much on food, however. Studies show that eating too little and excessive dieting contribute to insomnia.

Sometimes a light bedtime snack helps prevent midnight hunger, allowing you to sleep. Stay away from anything stimulating (chocolate cake) or hard to digest (pepperoni pizza). You might call room service for crackers and a small glass of milk (yes, a glass of milk can help you sleep—it's a natural sedative). Just don't overdo the fluids. While you should be drinking plenty of liquids, especially water, throughout the day, cut down on or eliminate fluids after 8 p.m. to prevent late-night trips to the bathroom.

For the business traveler, alcohol, caffeine, and nicotine wreak havoc on good sleep. "Business people are drinking a lot of coffee and alcohol on the plane and then they don't understand why they can't sleep," says Dr. Clerk. Many travelers use alcohol as a sleep aid, but that extra nightcap will not help you sleep, says Dr. Clerk. While you may drift off for a time, your sleep will be lighter and fragmented, with many awakenings. One glass of wine at an early dinner probably will not stick around long enough to hurt your sleep, but try to limit your drinking—and don't drink at all within two hours before bedtime.

Caffeine and tobacco are both stimulants. "Caffeine has been shown to cause people to take longer to get to sleep, to cause more awakenings, and to lower the quality of sleep, even in people who are not aware of it," writes Dr. Hauri. He advises that more than three cups of coffee or cola a day are likely to adversely affect sleep. For some people, one cup of coffee will disrupt sleep. While you may not be ready to give up caffeine completely, try to limit your consumption (even if you did not sleep the night before!). Avoid caffeine alto-gether—in coffee, tea, chocolate, or cola—within five to six hours before bedtime. You should note that many medications, including analgesics, cold medications, and diet pills, contain caffeine.

Nicotine also is a powerful stimulant, and studies show that smokers take longer to fall asleep and have more disturbed sleep than non-smokers. Impaired sleep is just another good reason to kick the habit. If you're still mustering your willpower to quit, don't light up near bedtime—you will just invite insomnia.

## Discard Distorted Beliefs

After counting the cracks in the hotel room's ceiling for what seems like an eternity, your mind begins obsessing with thoughts of disaster: "If I don't sleep, tomorrow's presentation will fail." "I won't be able to function." "I must have eight hours of sleep." "If I miss another night's sleep, I'll die."

Allowing distorted thoughts of this nature to run wild virtually guarantees a sleepless night. How you think about sleep will affect how you sleep. You don't want to associate sleeping with angry, anxious thoughts or become obsessed with the idea of sleep. The next time you can't sleep, and your mind races with thoughts of doom, remember that while you might not feel great the next day, you will live. With the excitement of being in a new place, the odds are that you will have enough adrenaline to get through the next day just fine, whether you slept well or not.

## When You Can't Sleep, Get Out of Bed

If you are not asleep within 15 to 20 minutes, get out of bed. *Never try to sleep!* The more you try to sleep, the more sleep will elude you. Sleep doctors tell of chronic insomniacs who were cured when they were asked for a time to deliberately try *not* sleeping. The sheer relief of not having to sleep freed them to sleep.

Getting out of bed breaks the "can't sleep" cycle. Try stretching quietly for five to ten minutes, or read a book. If you really feel anxious, take out some paper and list your top worries. Sometimes externalizing our anxieties in this way frees us to sleep. Do not rework tomorrow's speech, however. The goal is to engage in relaxing activi-ties. When you feel yourself becoming drowsy, try to sleep again. Repeat the process until you get to sleep.

## Take Power Naps

Most of us feel a little guilty when we nap. "Naps to most people mean you're lazy, stupid, or can't keep up. We're trying hard to dispel that notion," says Dr. Rosekind at NASA. "Getting some sleep when you're traveling is always better than no sleep."

The trick, says Dr. Rosekind, is to trust your own physiology. If you arrive in London after a 10-hour flight and cannot stay awake in the cab ride back to the hotel, don't fight it. Take a short nap.

Your body will tell you when it's a good time to nap. Your natural rhythm hits two low points during the day. For most of us, the points of maximal sleepiness arrive between 3 p.m. and 5 p.m., and 4 a.m. and 5 a.m. A short nap in the afternoon can really recharge your battery. If you're in a new time zone, nap when you would be tired on your home time. There are, however, some "smart napping" rules to follow.

Limit your nap to 45 minutes or shorter, advises Dr. Rosekind. You want to cut the nap off before entering the really deep stages of sleep so that you awake refreshed, he says. The goal is to boost your alertness, not to replace a good night's sleep. If you nap for a longer time, you run the risk of interfering with your nighttime sleep and your ability to beat jet lag after a long transmeridian flight. Never rely on napping to eliminate your sleep debt. Moreover, never nap after 4 p.m. local time; it might keep you up at night. If you are a chronic insomniac, however, it is probably best not to nap at all. Instead, focus on getting a good night's sleep.

## Schedule Worry Time

Limit worry time to 30 minutes a day or less, and make an appointment with yourself to "worry" early in the day. During your worry time, sit down and list everything that is really bothering you. Then write down an action plan for each item to make worry time become solution time. This technique prevents you from waiting until you are trying to sleep to mull over your problems.

## Be Prepared!

Whether you are traveling to participate in a key meeting or to pitch your services to a new client, prepare well in advance for any business you will conduct on the trip. Procrastination is a sleep robber. You will either be up late preparing or you will be too anxious to sleep.

## TRAVEL FITNESS TIPS: THE ART OF AIRPORT NAPPING

With substantial time between connecting flights, and all too many delayed or canceled flights, you may spend more time than you want at airport terminals. Catching a short catnap is a healthy way to pass the time, but how do you do it? Those upright airport chairs with armrests that will not lift up aren't exactly conducive to sleep. Here is what some of the frequent business travelers we spoke with suggested:

- Ask at the information desk if the airport has someplace to sleep—a couch in a private room or just a place to spread out away from the crowd. There's no harm in asking.

- Check to see if the terminal has sleeping rooms you can rent. For example, LAX runs by concession a dollhouse-like hotel for the weary traveler called Skytel in its Tom Bradley terminal. Skytel rents rooms by the half hour up to eight hours. Each room is air conditioned, sound-proof, and out-fitted with a small bed, shower, telephone, and television. Rates range from $8.95 for a half hour to $47 for eight hours.

- Scout around for a place to "go horizontal"—maybe in an unused gate away from other people.

- As a last resort, sleep sitting up. Prop an elbow on the armrest and hold your head in your hand. It's not ideal, but you may get some rest.

- Wear comfortable clothes that are conducive to sleep.

"There's nothing like superb preparation to ease the restlessness and anxiety over how the trip is going to go," says Dr. Bagshaw. So prepare well and sleep great.

## To Medicate or Not: The Traveler's Dilemma

You should resist the temptation of popping pills to induce sleep. Sleep medication will not cure your traveler's insomnia. It will not reset your biological clock, give you good sleep habits, or prevent the stresses which keep you awake on the road.

Increasingly, sleep doctors recommend sleeping pills only for short-term and limited use, if at all. Most experts advise never taking more than one a week. (If you will be away two weeks, take only two pills with you so you will not be tempted to overdo it).

"Try good sleep hygiene first," advises Dr. Clerk. "One pill won't hurt, but if you use one or two on the road, and then more when you get back home to adjust, it's becoming a problem. If you're traveling every month, you'll have developed a really bad habit."

While the pills may induce sleep, they can quickly lose their effectiveness, and the quality of your sleep will be impaired. That's because sleep medication suppresses REM dreaming and prevents you from getting the truly deep sleep you need. You may wake up feeling worse than if you had tossed and turned all night. You may even wake up feeling like you have a hangover. Sleeping pills also cause a nasty side effect called "rebound insomnia," in which insomnia charges back, even worsens, when the pills are taken away. Fears of rebound insomnia keep many people addicted to sleep medication and escalate the risks of increased use.

If you decide to take sleeping pills, make sure your doctor prescribes one that works rapidly and has little carry-over to the next day. Every sleeping pill operates differently. For example, Ambien, which was recently introduced, is short-acting, produces a more normal sleep, and has fewer side effects compared to other sleep medication.

Studies show that behavioral changes work better than pills in the long run, so try the techniques outlined in this chapter before asking your doctor to write a prescription. There are healthier ways to combat traveler's insomnia.

# When to Seek Help

Most traveler's insomnia is transient or short-term, with disrupted sleep not lasting more than three weeks. If, however, your traveler's insomnia has graduated from a short-term problem to a chronic condition—you're having problems sleeping on the road and at home—you may want to speak with your doctor or seek a referral to a sleep disorders clinic. There may be a more serious medical or psychological problem causing your insomnia.

Here are some signs that you may need help:

- Your sleep difficulties have not improved after several weeks despite your best efforts.
- You're in a pattern of sleeping for eight to ten hours, and still feel extremely sleepy during the day.
- Your sleep problems are affecting your job or relationship.
- You believe your sleep is abnormal in some way. Maybe you are experiencing breathing difficulties, loud snoring, or unusual body movements.

The National Sleep Foundation maintains a list of accredited sleep centers around the country. The foundation estimates that 1,100 to 1,200 centers are operating nationwide. For a list of centers near you, write to the foundation at 122 South Robertson Boulevard, Third Floor, Los Angeles, CA 90048.

Remember, most travelers find relief from their sleep problems—so get the help you need. Sweet dreams!

## The Sleep Checklist

❏ Identify the cause(s) of your on-the-road insomnia.
❏ Reduce your sleep debt before leaving.
❏ Maintain a good sleep pattern at home.
❏ Make your hotel room into a sleep-conducive environment.
❏ Don't try to sleep unless you're drowsy.
❏ Observe bedtime rituals.
❏ Exercise.
❏ Eat light.
❏ Don't drink liquids after 8 p.m.
❏ Avoid alcohol, caffeine, and nicotine.
❏ Don't obsess about not sleeping.
❏ If you're tossing and turning, get out of bed.
❏ Take power naps.
❏ Limit your worry time to 30 minutes a day.
❏ Prepare for your trip.
❏ Learn to manage your travel stress.

# Taking Your Workout on the Road

> *"There's nothing more important than exercise on the road. It's one of the only healthy outlets you have."*
>
> Ellen Hollander
> frequent traveler from
> Washington, DC

**W**e all know that regularly exercising on the road will boost our well-being, but how many of us actually do it? According to a recent survey of frequent travelers by *USA Today*, 49% of respondents said they were in worse shape because of business travel. The same percentage reported they exercise less on the road than at home. Not having a familiar place to work out, poor workout facilities, high guest-user fees, changing time zones, frantic schedules, and reduced energy reserves get the better of many fitness-minded travelers. Probably the most common excuse is "I'm too heavily programmed when I'm on the road. I don't have the time and something has to go." Too often the thing that goes is exercise. But workouts are even more important while traveling to combat extra calories, jet lag, and stress. What's more, if you neglect your exercise while away, you run the risk of losing your hard-earned fitness gains. To be worthwhile, a fitness routine requires consistency. Gains in aerobic capacity, strength, muscle tone, and agility aren't magically frozen in time until you return from a trip. They start to erode when you're away and don't exercise.

Everyone can find the time and energy to exercise on the road. It doesn't require two hours a day in the hotel's health club to maintain the many fitness benefits of exercise. Even a 10-minute walk twice a day can get you on the road to feeling better.

Your job is to commit to making exercise an integral part of every trip. Once you decide that you're not going to sacrifice your exercise routine while traveling, you'll begin to see creative possibilities for accomplishing it. You'll view the logistics of getting it done more as a creative challenge than an insurmountable obstacle.

In this chapter, we'll help you negotiate the many challenges of working out while away. We'll give you tips for goal setting and researching fitness options, share six key travel workout principles, outline four creative workouts, and provide strategies for safety and working out while abroad. But first, let's assess how you're doing on the road. Take the following quiz to test your travel workout readiness quotient. Give yourself one point for each "yes" answer.

## Travel Workout Quiz

Circle *yes* or *no* next to these 18 statements. Then tally the number of "yes" responses and interpret your score on the next page.

<u>Circle one</u>

1. I always make time for my workout when traveling.  yes  no

2. When packing for a trip, I remember to pack workout  yes  no
   clothing and equipment.

3. I often take the stairs instead of an escalator or  yes  no
   elevator.

4. Before my trip, I check to see what health club amenities will be available at my hotel.  yes  no

5. I take special precautions to avoid injury while working out on the road.  yes  no

6. I know how to exercise within the confines of my hotel room.     yes     no

7. When pressed for time on the road, I usually attempt to at least get minimal exercise each day.     yes     no

8. My regular workout is adaptable to travel situations.     yes     no

9. I capitalize on a new environment to give me fresh workout ideas.     yes     no

10. While traveling, I stretch several times a day.     yes     no

11. I often incorporate fitness activities into business entertaining.     yes     no

12. I set realistic on-the-road fitness goals.     yes     no

13. I have developed methods to stay motivated to work out while traveling.     yes     no

14. I keep track of the progress I make with my on-the-road exercise goals.     yes     no

15. I have created 2-3 interchangeable travel workouts.     yes     no

16. When traveling, I frequently work out in the morning to make sure I get it in.     yes     no

17. I often make fitness a part of my sightseeing activities.     yes     no

18. On extended trips, I always make sure to get strength training *and* aerobic exercise.     yes     no

TOTAL     ___     ___

Score

1-6     Travel exacts a toll on your fitness well-being. Follow the tips in this chapter to improve your on-the-road workouts.

7-12     Travel is still harder on your fitness routine than it needs to be, but you are taking steps in the right direction.

13-18     You are handling the challenges of working out on the road and probably feel better than most travelers. But keep reading to discover other ways to improve.

# What's Your Excuse?

How many times have you slept through the hotel's alarm instead of rising early to squeeze in a workout? Felt too tired or busy to exercise on the road? Opted to drink with colleagues instead of playing tennis or golf? Travel provides a wealth of excuses if you're looking for them. "I have a theory on life that we always find the time to do the things we like to do and never have the time to do the things we don't like to do," David Chamberlain, Shaklee U.S. Inc's chairman, is quoted as saying in a recent interview. Chamberlain maintains a competitive schedule of working out four times a week even while traveling. "There isn't a Hyatt or Marriott that doesn't have a place to go and get a pretty good workout."

Instead of relegating your exercise routine to the back burner, confront the reasons why you don't exercise while traveling. Write down the obstacles which repeatedly dash your fitness plans and think of ways to get around them. Confront your excuses head-on. Are you really always too tired and overly scheduled on the road? Or are these rationalizations that sometimes reflect lack of commitment more than reality? Let's face it, keeping our exercise commitments, especially while traveling, requires hard work. When we look behind the "no time" or "too tired" excuses, often there's really little true justification for them.

Take lack of time. In some cases it's actually less time-consuming to work out on the road if you stay in a hotel with an exercise facility. "Getting in a workout is only an elevator ride away," says Wendy Paskin Jordan, 38, a banker with Montgomery Securities in San Francisco. "At home I have to make the effort to drive to the gym. But on the road I can get to the hotel gym in seconds."

Then there's fatigue. Many times the tiredness we feel while traveling comes from sitting too long in transit or in all-day meetings. Inactivity and boredom, not physical strain, usually make us feel bushed. Exercise is needed more than ever when we're feeling sluggish on the road—and all of us can find the time to walk or run for 15 to 20 minutes to energize ourselves.

One way to get past our resistance is to focus on the benefits of exercising while away. Not only does exercise recharge our batteries and keep us fit, but it increases alertness and productivity, replenishes the body's oxygen needs after flying, resets the body's clock, saves the back by increasing circulation, helps get us to sleep, burns calories, and reduces stress.

## Creating a Game Plan

Someone once said, "If you don't know where you're going, you might end up someplace else." Developing a blueprint for working out on the road will prevent you from abandoning your fitness regimen and winding up out-of-shape and overweight. "Inconsistency is the death of any fitness program," says Dr. James Rippe of the University of Massachusetts Medical School, who travels six or seven days a month and always packs his running shoes. "People who travel a lot will have great difficulty staying fit unless they make a very specific game plan to maintain their fitness program on the road," he says. Rippe, who interviewed 1,100 CEOs in the top 1 to 2 percent for travel, says most of them plan their fitness regimen right along with the rest of the trip's itinerary.

If you're committed to making exercise a part of every trip, start by getting a handle on your long- and short-term fitness goals. Are you exercising to build strength, lose weight, or run a 10K in less than 40 minutes? What types and amounts of exercise do you plan on getting each week? Each month? Will you alternate between heavy and light training periods? Write them down. Once you've etched out the big picture, ask yourself: How will my travel workouts fit into my overall fitness plan? Can I schedule my trip during a light training week so I don't have to push myself too hard while away and still meet my goals? Be as specific and realistic as possible when setting goals. You need a reasonable chance of meeting your goals to stay motivated. Let's say, for example, that you've committed to running 20 miles a week to stay in shape. When the next four-day trip rolls around, scheduling two five-mile runs is a specific, achievable goal that allows you to meet your longer-term objective. It's better than departing with the vague idea of "getting some exercise," a notion which will soon evaporate once you set foot in the hotel's lounge. As a general rule, the more specific and goal-driven your travel workout regimen, the more likely you will actually do it.

Just knowing where you're headed with your on-the-road fitness program gives you the mental ammunition to resist slacking off. But you'll also need a specific plan for each trip to convert your goals to action. Take 10 to 15 minutes before you leave, or if you're a born procrastinator, on the plane, to do some exercise research and planning. Create a plan that works for you. Really visualize how you're going to get some exercise. Make it a point to schedule outdoor exercise, if possible, right after a long flight to help reset your clock and shake off the effects of travel. If you're going to run, what clothes or fitness gear will you need? Where will you do it, and when? If lap swimming is your exercise, book a lane at a local health club and pack your swim gear. Some folks plan their trips around a "fun run" or other sporting event. We recommend writing out the workouts you plan to accomplish and taking the plan with you. Your workout plan should be part of your overall personal travel health and fitness program discussed in Chapter 1.

One approach that works well for many of the travelers we interviewed is to schedule regular fitness appointments with yourself. Take out your pocket planner and *pencil in your workouts*, just like any other important meeting. If another request threatens to preempt your exercise appointment, say you're already busy at that time. For many, committing to a time slot ensures that it will get done.

When devising your trip-specific exercise plan, keep it as simple as possible. For example, if you're choosing among various aerobic exercises, choose one like walking or running that doesn't require special equipment. If your workout is too complicated, you won't do it. Also, build in social support whenever you can. By bringing another person into your exercise planning, you'll tap another great motivator—peer pressure. Ask your business contacts if they'll meet for a game of tennis, squash, or golf, or accompany you on a run or walk. You won't miss a minute of work that way. Or call a friend in the area and arrange to work out together. Paul Beirne, 32, partner at Sanford C. Bernstein, Inc. in New York, schedules an appointment with a personal trainer at his destination. "I found that working out with a trainer is important for me because I don't have that much self-discipline regarding exercise. I need someone to coax me on. I put the appointment right in my book like any other, and I keep it."

To help you keep to your goals, chart your progress. Keep records of your on-the-road exercise. Take note of the type, frequency, duration, and intensity of your workouts. Log the number of miles you walk or run. You might pack a pedometer to keep track of distance. How do you feel after working out? Do you have more energy? Are you better able to maintain your weight after increasing your exercise? Once you see that you're getting results—you feel better, you're sleeping better, you're shaving off excess pounds—you'll want to stay with it.

As you start on the road to fitness, avoid perfectionism. If you reach most of your fitness goals, you're doing just fine. For each goal reached, no matter how small, find a way to reward yourself. Take a hot sauna or get a massage. You deserve it.

## Strategies for Finding Fitness Options

To plan a travel exercise routine, you need to discover available workout opportunities at your destination. Most of the time, unearthing superb fitness options is only a phone call away. For traveling fitness buffs, the first order of business is locating a hotel with an on-site fitness facility and pool or with access to a nearby club. Ready access to a reasonably equipped fitness room is essential to maintaining an exercise routine. "I simply won't stay in a hotel that doesn't have a fitness club," says Mark Beirne, 34, a physician from Anchorage, Alaska, who plans all of his trips with exercise in mind. It shouldn't be too tough to find a club. About 40 percent of American hotels now offer some kind of fitness facility for their guests, according to a survey by the American Hotel and Motel Association, and an increasing number of Asian and European hotels also have facilities. When you're booking your room, remember, however, that not all hotel fitness facilities and pools are created equal. Most focus on cardiovascular equipment, which may be disappointing if contouring your muscles is a priority. If you're a serious weight trainer, you might be better off using a local Y. Many hotel clubs simply stretch the truth of what they offer. "My biggest gripe is going to a hotel that says it has a fitness room, and then you get there and find one bike that's 25 years old and a Universal gym that's rusting," says Tim Martineau, 35, a director with Price Waterhouse in Denver.

The hotel may offer more exercise options than a pool or fitness facility. Ask about outdoor fitness courses and access to good running trails. Many hotels provide jogging maps with distances marked. Some even have a running escort on staff to ensure safety or organize morning runs. For guests who are unwilling to brave a new exercise facility, many hotels will loan exercise videocassettes for use with in-room VCRs or provide other in-room options. The Meridien hotel chain, for example, offers a step-aerobics exercise routine played hourly on one of the hotel's channels as part of its STEP program. Guests just need to call housekeeping and request a platform.

What if you're booked in a hotel without an exercise facility or with only a marginal one? Not to worry. There are some simple tricks for gaining access to health clubs in a new area. Before leaving, find out if your health club has a reciprocal arrangement with any of the clubs at your destination. If your club is a member of IRSA, the association of quality clubs, you can gain access to more than 1,600 affiliated clubs in the United States and abroad through the Passport Program. Call (800) 766-1278 for information on participating clubs, or ask for the IRSA Passport Program's book. Most of the large franchised clubs like Gold's Gym or the YMCA also admit members to clubs across the country. Through the AWAY (Always Welcome at the Y) program, Y members can work out at facilities in the United

# TRAVEL FITNESS TIPS:
# HOTEL FITNESS FACILITY CHECKLIST

To avoid the disappointment of finding a fitness room that doesn't meet your needs, always call ahead and make some inquiries. The following form lists items to inquire about. Copy and use it before each trip. Keep the completed forms for future reference.

Hotel: _____ Phone: _____

Address: _____ Fax: _____

Contact person: _____

Hours of operation: _____

Peak hours of use: _____

On-site fitness supervisor: _____

Entry fee: _____

Access to personal trainer: _____

Charge/hr.: _____

Type & no. of strength equipment: _____

Type & no. of cardiovascular equipment: _____

Access to exercise classes: _____

Use of sauna, steam, Jacuzzi: _____

Access to running track: _____

Length of track: _____

Access to racquetball/tennis: _____

Access to basketball courts: _____

Use of pool (length, shape, how crowded, use of lap lane, temperature, in-service, indoor/outdoor): _____
_____

Amenities (lockers, towels, workout clothes, shampoo, soap):
_____

Access to challenge court: _____

States at minimal or no cost. Gold's Gym gives members a two-week pass, allowing them to work out at various locations in the United States and abroad at no cost.

Another way to gain non-resident admission to a club at your destination is through a fee-based club network. For example, by paying an annual fee to Associate Clubs International, Club Corporation of America ((800) 433-5079), members have access to more than 200 private country and city clubs and resorts around the world which offer golf courses, pools, and exercise facilities.

Keep in mind that many health clubs allow non-members to work out for a daily fee. If you regularly travel to a certain city or plan on an extended stay, inquire about temporary or part-time memberships at a local club. Many clubs will work with you and even waive the initiation fee.

If health clubs away from home seem less than inviting, get the skinny on other fitness options that appeal to you. Keep in mind your short- and long-term fitness goals, and research ways to achieve them. If you prefer working out in the privacy of your hotel room, ask a fitness instructor at your health club how to modify your routine for the road. You might even take your exercise routine card from your hometown club with you while traveling or have a personal trainer create an exercise audiotape to take with you. If you work out on your own, simply write down the exercises from your routine that could be done in your hotel room. Many of the basic, yet effective exercises—sit-ups, push-ups, lunges, stretches, running in place—can be done in your hotel room with no equipment. Outlined later in this chapter is a basic workout routine that can be done in any hotel room.

If running is your preferred exercise, do your homework. If the concierge at your hotel can't help you, peruse a runner's magazine or call local contacts—a sporting goods store, the Chamber of Commerce, the local recreation department, or the area runner's club—to find out about upcoming races and to locate a safe and interesting place to run. The American Running and Fitness Association (ARFA), 4405 East-West Highway, Suite 405, Bethesda, MD 20814, (301) 913-9517, operates the Exercise Trails Network. For $1, ARFA will recommend running or walking trails at your destination. If all else fails, veteran traveler Bill Wood, 40, of Harrison, Maine, offers this solution: "I do laps around the motel," he says. "I've found that five times around the typical Motel 6 equals about a mile. I run around the motel 20 times to get my four miles in. It's kind of boring but at least I'm exercising."

A little planning can add to your walking excursions as well. "I find someone knowledgeable about the local area to help me plan an early morning fitness walk," says fitness expert Sandra Fisher. "I like to find an historic area that's safe. Planning ahead makes all the difference."

Other aerobic options to explore include renting outdoor equipment like bikes, rollerblades, cross-country skis, or ice skates; or finding local tennis courts or pools. When Melissa Price traveled to Chicago in the summer, she rented rollerblades and skated for two or three hours every night after work. "I needed to compensate for the lack of activity all day," she says. "On the road, I'm flexible. I find exercise wherever I can."

# Six Key Principles for Working Out on the Road

Regardless of the exercise options you choose, keep in mind these travel fitness principles while on the road.

## 1. Listen to Your Body

After a grueling journey, our bodies can be in a mild state of shock. Changes in altitude, time zones, stiff muscles from sitting in a plane or car, and general fatigue all increase the risk of injury while exercising. Common sense dictates that we shouldn't run a marathon immediately after arriving at a destination. But what is the right amount of exercise? The answer is different for each of us and depends on interpreting the cues our bodies send us.

Experts advise avoiding rigorous exercise for the first 24 hours after arrival to give the body time to adjust. "After long-distance traveling and crossing different time zones, if you're just so tired that you feel it violates good judgment to work out, then don't," says Dr. Rippe. The cardinal rule of exercising on the road is "go slow," says John Duncan, Ph.D., an exercise physiologist and chief of clinical application at the Cooper Institute for Aerobics Research in Dallas. "If you're working out on exercise equipment, maybe start out with half the workload you normally would do and slowly work yourself back up," he says.

Before doing anything ask yourself: What type and level of exercise will give me the benefits I want without overdoing it? Learning to determine how much is too much requires listening to your body. If you've traveled a long way, we suggest making your first exercise session easy. Focus more on stretching and light aerobic activity like brisk walking or swimming in the hotel pool instead of heavy-duty weight training. Mark Beirne usually cuts back on the length and intensity of his workouts when he travels. "When I get through my warm-up and it's pooping me out, I know I need to slow down," he says.

As you exercise, if something begins to hurt or cause excessive fatigue, slow down or stop. If discomfort persists, take time off from your program and consult with a trainer or physician.

## 2. Maintain a Balanced Fitness Program on the Road

A balanced fitness program includes aerobic, strength, and flexibility training. Ideally your at-home routine already incorporates these three fitness components. Don't lose sight of these goals on the road.

Focus your travel workouts in a way that mirrors what you're already doing at home. Maintaining at least a semblance of an at-home routine creates structure and familiarity, two requisites to feeling better and more connected while away. Being on the road is no time to transform yourself into a jock, however. If you're running ten miles a week at home, don't try for twenty miles on the road.

Whatever blend of activities you use to achieve your specific fitness objectives, try to replicate them on the road. If you've been cross-training at home, you'll find it easier to find suitable options while away. For example, if you regularly bike, row, and jog at home, you may find it easier just to jog while traveling. But aim to increase the amount of time you spend stretching and warming up. "Whether you're flying or sitting in long meetings, travel increases the amount of time spent in a chair. Your muscles are tighter," says Dr. Bagshaw. "If you're going to work out, a longer warm-up makes sense."

Honoring the proper sequence of exercising is even more important when working out on the road. To maximize the benefits of exercise and reduce the risk of injury, the National Exercise for Life Institute recommends this order of exercise activity (this sequence is essential to follow on the road):

1. Four to five minutes of low level aerobic activity as a warm-up
2. Stretching
3. Aerobic conditioning
4. Cool down
5. Strength training
6. Stretching

If one part of your routine has to go, don't let it be aerobic training, says Dr. Rippe. "The cornerstone of any fitness program, and the one that has been shown to relieve stress, is aerobic conditioning. If travelers can commit to that and develop a good routine of stretching around it, they won't suffer too much on the road," he says.

## 3. Use It or Lose It

Many people who have regular workout routines worry about losing fitness benefits if they don't exercise while traveling—for good reason. The benefits of exercise don't last. Unfortunately, the more fit you are, the more you have to lose.

A drop-off in physical conditioning is referred to as the "decay curve." If you do nothing whatsoever, your fitness level starts to decrease in seven to ten days, says Neil Gordon, M.D., Ph.D. If you subjected an athlete to strict bed rest, every seven days his or her aerobic capacity would decrease the same amount as it would with 10 years of aging! "If we just stop training, but are up and about, our fitness level decreases, but not to the same degree," he says.

Aerobic conditioning is the first element of fitness to suffer from inactivity. After about two weeks of not exercising, about 10 percent of aerobic capacity is lost. After four to eight weeks, you're back to square one. "If you trained for 20 years and then take off four to eight weeks, your aerobic fitness level is going to be back to what it was 21 years ago," says Dr. Duncan. Strength lasts a bit longer; it takes between eight and ten weeks to lose an appreciable amount.

Don't panic at the specter of losing your fitness level on the road. You can do less for a time and still stay in shape. According to Dr. Gordon, research has shown that a person can maintain all of his or her hard-earned fitness benefits for up to three weeks by following three rules during the period of reduced activity.

Rule No. 1: Exercise at least every third day. "If you can't exercise every day, it's not the end of the world, but you do want to be exercising at least every third day," Dr. Gordon says.

Rule No. 2: You can cut the length of the aerobic portion of your routine by two-thirds but you must keep the intensity the same. For example, if you jog at a nine-minute-mile pace for 45 minutes at home, you must jog for at least 15 minutes at the same pace on the road.

Rule No. 3:  Do your strength training program at least once a week, using the same amount of resistance.

"Even with an elite athlete, studies show that you can cut the duration and frequency of an exercise program by as much as two-thirds for up to three weeks and still preserve your fitness level if you keep the intensity of the workout the same," Dr. Gordon says. "In a sense you're giving your body a chance to recuperate and yet getting in enough physiologic stimulus to prevent you from losing benefits." Of course, you can't be on this reduced program three weeks out of every month and still expect to be at your peak, he says.

## 4. While Traveling, Be Creative and Flexible With Your Workouts

Keeping an open mind and being willing to try something new will help you maintain your fitness level while traveling. "Travelers have to be more creative in finding time and ways to stay active," says David Jackson, an exercise physiologist at the University of South Carolina. The good news is that being in a new environment provides numerous opportunities to diversify your exercise regime—if you take the time to look for them. Why not take a class at the hotel's golf school after work, or try a yoga class? Traveling to different climates also opens up fitness options. Travel to a warm place creates an opening for tennis, water sports, bike riding, or rollerblading. Heading to a cold climate means ice skating and cross-country skiing. "Anyone who travels a lot has to be a chameleon. That way, you get the most of what every city has to offer," says Barbara Wambach, a San Francisco-based traveler. While traveling to the Far East, Wambach takes advantage of state-of-the-art health clubs. In Florence, Italy, where she has yet to find a good gym, she walks or rents a bike. In resort locations, she opts for water sports like scuba diving or wind surfing. "Your exercise routine must be flexible to where you are," she says.

Many of the frequent travelers we interviewed found ingenious ways to sneak in exercise on the road. For example, Ellen Hollander hired a personal trainer to design two workout routines for her to use while traveling. One routine aims to help her obtain a maximum workout from an incomplete hotel facility. The other is a workout she can do in a standard hotel room, making do with what's in the room. The routine includes triceps and biceps exercises using books or lamps found in any hotel room, along with push-ups, sit-ups, and other basic exercises that can be performed anywhere. Other travelers

# TRAVEL FITNESS TIPS:
# 10 GREAT RUNNING CITIES

We asked Doug Rennie, an avid runner and a writer who critiques travel destinations for *Runner's World*, to share his picks for 10 great cities for runners. If you're traveling to one of these cities, get out and enjoy the trails.

- **Portland, Oregon:** A mild climate year-round; running trails along the Willamette River, mere blocks from city center; and 27 miles of rolling, creek-crossed trails in Forest Park, five minutes from downtown; make this a runner's paradise.

- **Washington, DC:** From the crushed granite pathways of the Capitol Mall and the paved paths of West Potomac Park that wind past the Jefferson, Lincoln, and Vietnam Memorials; to the streamside trails of Rock Creek Park, the historic Mt. Vernon bike path, and the dirt paths along the C&O Canal; no city offers a greater variety of running options.

- **San Diego, California:** The best weather anywhere; a flat, 10-mile running loop around Mission Bay; and rugged off-road running in Balboa Park just minutes from downtown; make this a great runner's destination.

- **San Francisco, California:** Pluses include miles of bike and nature trails in Golden Gate Park, a great run from Fisherman's Wharf along the Bay to the Golden Gate Bridge, and cool marine air virtually every day of the year.

- **Vancouver, British Columbia:** Just 10 minutes from downtown, Stanley Park offers many scenic options from a six-mile run along the Seawall perimeter to trails and paths that crisscross the park's interior, past secluded Beaver Lake and Lost Lagoon, a serene bird sanctuary.

- **Minneapolis, Minnesota:** Winter months aside, Minny offers great trails around each of its three in-town lakes (each about three miles around), just minutes west of downtown; along the Minnehaha Parkway, south of city center; and the bluff trails above the Mississippi River.

- **Honolulu, Hawaii:** It's always warm to hot and humid, but this city offers everything from shady and flat trails (Kapiolani Park loop) to eye-popping scenic (around Diamond Head) to jungle-like (the Tantalus Trail 10 minutes from downtown).
- **Boulder, Colorado:** Just about every run here is challenging—from the rugged, rolling Mesa Trail along the base of the Flatiron Mountains to the tough Switzerland Trail that offers vistas of the Rockies and the Continental Divide. In town, the popular Boulder Creek Path snakes its peaceful, wooded way through the city.
- **Atlanta, Georgia:** Urban Piedmont Park is a runner-friendly, tree-lined triangle (just under 3 miles around). The river-silt nature trails along the Chattahoochee River (10 minutes northwest of the city) are always buzzing with runners.
- **Boston, Massachusetts:** The paved bike paths along both the Boston and Cambridge sides of the Charles River make up a 17.2-mile loop (with great views of the Boston skyline and Harvard rowing crews), but numerous bridges allow you to choose the distance of your run.

use the hotel stairs as a substitute for a step machine, pack portable exercise equipment, power-walk through local malls, and even jog through the hotel hallways. Says veteran traveler Jose Perez, 26, of Atlanta, whose exercise routine includes tennis, racquetball, running, and lifting weights: "You have to just do whatever is available at your destination."

Alternating activities on the road keeps you in shape and offers two key cross-training benefits: the opportunity to work different muscle groups and break the monotony of routine. "Variety is important," says Dr. Gordon. "It keeps your program more interesting. It keeps you more motivated."

Let's say, for example, that you're training for a 10K. If on a business trip, you could swim laps in a club pool, getting great cardiovascular exercise, improving your aerobic capacity for running, but also working out your upper body for a change. But, warns Dr. Gordon, don't overdo it and wind up injured. Requiring medical care away from home because of an injury or suffering from sore muscles shouldn't be the consequence of working out on the road. "You don't want to go out and do a different exercise every day. Instead try to have more than one exercise at your disposal that you've done at some point before and use them to cross train," says Gordon, who jogs and uses a stationary cycle when traveling.

## 5. Something Is Better Than Nothing

We've all heard the axiom that you have to work out at least 20 minutes per session to benefit from aerobic exercise. Many a traveler has put exercise on hold, waiting for a sufficient block of time, which too often never materializes. But not having enough time isn't an excuse any longer. New studies show that a regular, moderate amount of activity, spread throughout the course of a day, will keep you healthy. Even three 10-minute sessions of moderate intensity exercise a day can improve cardiovascular fitness and help you lose weight. The goal of 20 to 30 minutes of high-intensity aerobic activity three or more times a week is no longer the minimum exercise mandate. 1993 guidelines from the American College of Sports Medicine, the Centers for Disease Control and Prevention, and the President's Council on Physical Fitness and Sports advocate accumulating 30 minutes or more of moderate-intensity physical activity over the course of most days of the week.

Few people are too busy to accrue 30 minutes of activity every day. It's potentially as simple as walking briskly to meetings, taking the hotel stairs instead of the elevator, or jogging in place in your hotel room. Later in the chapter we offer tips for achieving the "no-time" workout.

## 6. Get It Done in the A.M.

When planning your on-the-road exercise, keep in mind that the earlier in the day you schedule it, the more likely you're going to get it done. The reason is simple: nothing will get in your way. Even on the busiest trip, how much is usually scheduled between 6:30 a.m. and 8 a.m.? By getting up 30 to 45 minutes earlier and going for a walk or heading to the hotel gym, your exercise plans won't be waylaid by long meetings or last-minute scheduling changes later in the day. In fact, studies show that people who work out first thing in the morning are more consistent over the long-term with exercise. Nearly all of the CEOs interviewed by Dr. Rippe worked out early in the morning. "They found through bitter experience that their day started falling apart if they didn't do it first thing in the morning," says Dr. Rippe. What's more, a morning workout is a great metabolism booster. And getting outdoors for some exercise in the morning sunlight will help reset your jet-lagged biological clock.

Of course your body needs to cooperate in your plans. Timing workouts is an individual thing. There are larks and owls. If rising early to work up a sweat is about as appealing as joining the folks who cut back the ice on some frigid lake each winter to go for a swim, remember the best workout time is the time you'll actually do it.

If you do elect a morning workout, follow the exercise sequence outlined on page 107. Absolutely avoid stretching too intensely when you're cold. "You have to be very careful with a.m. workouts in terms of flexibility," Jackson says. Your muscles shorten at night, creating a greater risk of certain injuries in the morning. Move around a little bit first. Take a short walk, jog in place, or do some jumping jacks. Then start to stretch.

# Four Creative On-the-Road Workouts

The next few pages detail four workouts you might want to try the next time you're on the road.

## Workout #1: The No-Time Workout

When there's not a gym in sight or you're too busy for structured exercise, incorporate this no-time workout into your travel schedule. The goal: to accrue 30 minutes of aerobic activity and 10 minutes of stretching across the span of each day that you're away. The key to this workout is finding those hidden opportunities throughout your day to squeeze in a few creative exercises or stretches. Choose to be active whenever and wherever you can. Think in small segments and recognize that every bit of activity counts toward your goals.

Develop the mindset that your workout begins as soon as you leave. "From the minute I leave my house, I place increased emphasis on working physical activity into my routine. I'll park towards the end of the airport's parking lot, and I'll walk carrying my bags. I avoid moving sidewalks. I keep walking as I go up an escalator. I try to take the stairs whenever I can," says Dr. Gordon, who does his own version of the no-time workout while traveling.

Increase your time spent walking whenever possible. Book a hotel near where you'll be working so you can walk to and from meetings.

Walk to and from restaurants. Avoid taxis. Take a walking tour of the city in the evening. Jimmy Gray, 62, a sales representative from Nashville, tells us what he does. "Instead of hassling to find a parking place right in front of my customer's business, I park two or three blocks away and walk to the meeting. That way, I spread my exercise throughout the day." For an added pump, take the stairs: it's one of the quickest ways to get vigorous aerobic exercise, the kind that boosts your metabolism and increases your alertness. Try doing the push-pull arm isometric exercises outlined in Chapter 2 while climbing. This allows you to exercise your upper and lower body at the same time.

Don't allow yourself to sit in a chair for more than 40 to 50 minutes. Use every chance to stand up, walk around, and stretch. "I think we have a concept about meeting structures where we become fixed features. We're supposed to be glued to the chair, we're supposed to stay in a certain physical relationship to the room," says James Gavin, a sports psychologist, professor of applied social science at Concordia University, and author of *The Exercise Habit* (1992). "People need to just get up in long meetings and do whatever movement they need to do to stay energized," he says. You can, for example, work your quadriceps by getting out of your chair using one leg only or by standing near your chair in a slightly bent-leg position. No one will be the wiser. If you're trapped sitting for more than a half hour, try some of the seated exercises outlined in Chapter 2, which can be performed inconspicuously in your chair.

Look for opportunities to accumulate 10 minutes or more of stretching during the day. Seize opportunities to stretch while watching TV in your hotel room, riding alone in an elevator, waiting in line, or at other semi-private times.

# ■ *The No-Time Stretches*

Here are six "no-time" stretches that can be performed easily at intervals throughout the day.

### 1. Calf Stretch
Stand facing a wall or other structure. While keeping the heel of your right foot on the ground, lift the ball of your right foot as high as it will go and place it against the wall. Keeping your right leg and body straight, lean into the wall. Hold the calf stretch for several seconds. Repeat with the left foot.

| 1. Calf Stretch | 2. Standing Quadricep Stretch |
| --- | --- |
|  | 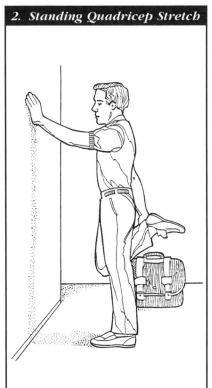 |

### 2. Standing Quadricep Stretch

Standing straight, hold your right ankle with your right hand. Place your left hand on a wall or chair for balance. Pull up on your right leg until you feel a stretch in your quadriceps. Hold for several seconds. Repeat with the opposite leg.

### 3. Hamstring Stretch

Using a chair, bench, or any object approximately three to four feet high, place the heel of your right foot on the "platform," with your leg extended straight in front of your body. Slowly drop your chest towards your leg, stretching your right hamstring muscle. Keep your back straight and your pelvis in a neutral alignment. Hold for several seconds. Repeat with the opposite leg (see page 44 for an illustration).

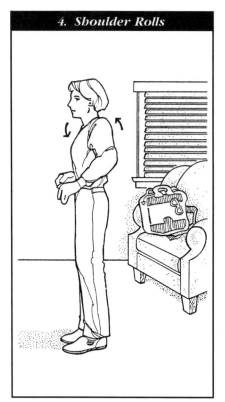

### 4. *Shoulder Rolls*

Roll both shoulders forward in a circular motion five times. Then reverse direction. You may stand or sit to perform this stretch.

### 5. *Shoulder-Arm Stretch*

Stand with your right side facing a wall and your right arm extended straight, touching the wall at shoulder level. Keep your right hand on the wall. Gradually turn your body counter-clockwise until you feel a stretch in your right arm and shoulder. Hold for 4-5 seconds. Reverse the stretch by standing with your left side facing a wall with your left arm extended and left hand touching the wall at shoulder level. Then turn clockwise until you feel the stretch in your left arm and shoulder. Hold 4-5 seconds.

### 6. *Full Body Stretch*

In the standing position, raise both arms above your head and raise yourself up onto your toes. Reach up as high as you can, feeling the stretch throughout your entire body. Hold for 3-4 seconds.

## Workout #2: The Express Hotel Room Workout

Look at your hotel room as a private gym away from home. Below we've outlined a balanced fitness exercise program combining stretching, strength, and aerobic conditioning called the Express Hotel Room Workout. The exercises described work each major muscle group. Before starting the routine, rearrange furniture in your room as needed for extra space.

Begin the routine with a 4- to 5-minute warm-up by jogging slowly in place. Next, stretch for 4-5 minutes. Perform the No-Time Stretches above or your own stretching routine. Now you're ready to start the Express Hotel Room Workout. Do the exercises below in sequence, adjusting the number of repetitions to your fitness level. Between each set, add an aerobic component for 30 to 60 seconds. We suggest jogging in place or jumping rope. After completing the workout, stretch to cool down for 4-5 minutes. This workout can be completed in 20 to 30 minutes.

# ❚ *Middle Body Exercises*

### *1. Crunches*

Lie on your back with your feet flat on the floor and your knees bent. Cross your arms over your chest. Using your abdominal muscles, pull your chest to your knees. Repeat 15-25 times.

## 2. Back Arches

Lying on your stomach, use your lower back muscles to lift your shoulders off the ground and back as far as you can towards your feet. Keep your feet on the ground and your arms at your sides. Use your arms (as in a push-up) as necessary to raise your shoulders from the ground. Repeat 8-20 times.

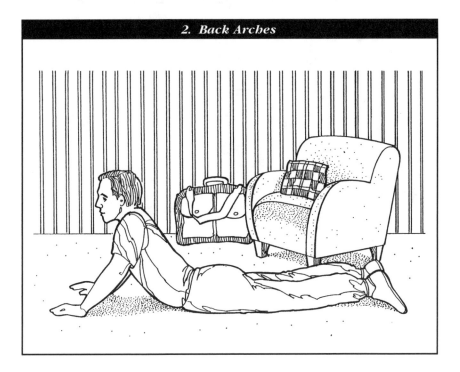

2. Back Arches

### 3. Arm-Leg Raises

Lying on your stomach, lift your left arm and right leg. Hold for one or two seconds and lower. Repeat 8-20 times. Perform the same exercise by lifting your right arm and left leg. Repeat 8-20 times.

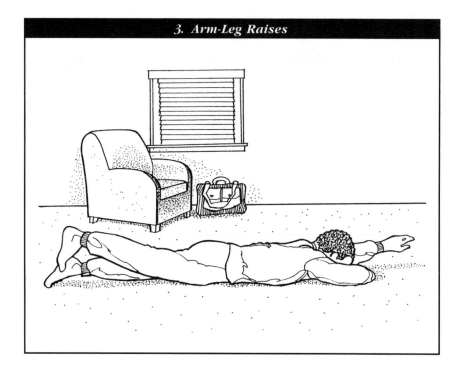

**3. Arm-Leg Raises**

# ▮ *Lower Body Exercises*

### *1. Squats*

Stand erect with your feet placed shoulder-width apart. With your back straight and your pelvis in a neutral alignment, bend your knees to almost 90 degrees. Then stand upright. Try to keep your rib cage lifted and your abdominal muscles tucked in throughout the movement. Repeat 8-20 times.

*1. Squats*

## 2. Lunges

Stand with your back straight and pelvis in neutral alignment. Place your left foot a comfortable distance in front of you. Bend both knees and lower your body until your right knee almost touches the floor. Keep your rib cage lifted and abdominal muscles contracted throughout the motion. Return to the standing position. Repeat 8-20 times. Perform the same exercise with the right leg in front. Repeat 8-20 times.

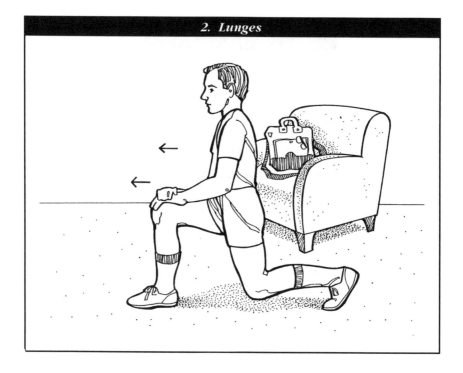

2. Lunges

### 3. Hamstring Isometrics

Lie flat on your back on the hotel room bed, with your feet extended just over the edge. Press your heels, back of legs and buttock down into the bed by squeezing your hamstring muscles. Hold for 4-5 seconds. Repeat 10 times.

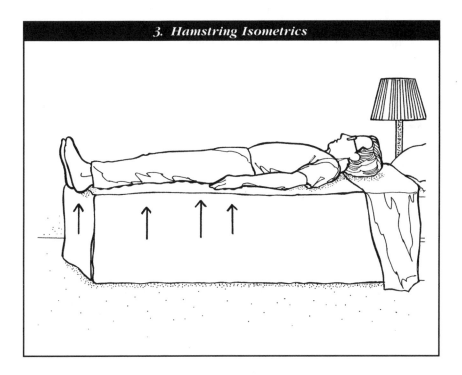

*3. Hamstring Isometrics*

### 4. Calf Raises

Using one hand to balance yourself, simply raise both heels from the floor and hold yourself upright on the balls of your feet (see illustration on page 44). Release. Repeat 5-10 times. To increase difficulty, raise yourself on one foot at a time or use a phone book or other thick book for greater range of motion.

# ▌ *Upper Body Exercises*

### 1. Push-Ups

Lie on the floor with your body straight. With your weight distributed between your hands and the balls of your feet, raise your body until your arms are almost straight. Slowly, bend your elbows and lower your chest until it almost touches the floor. Keep your body straight throughout the motion. Repeat 8-20 times.

For a less difficult variation, keep your knees on the floor while performing the push-up. The back should be kept straight during either type of push-up.

### 2. Seated or Standing Curls

Keep a comfortable amount of weight in your briefcase or piece of luggage. Stand straight with your briefcase in your left hand. With your elbow tucked close to your side, bend your arm and raise the briefcase to chest height. Lower and repeat 8-20 times. Switch the briefcase to your right hand and repeat 8-20 times. If you prefer, you can perform this exercise while seated.

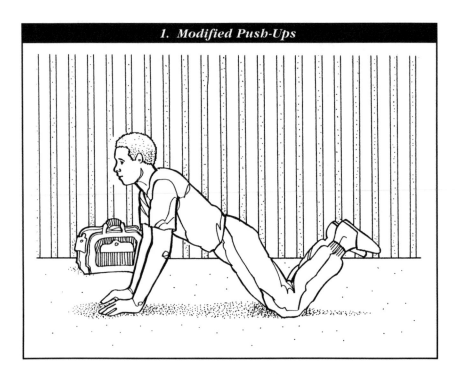

**1. Modified Push-Ups**

### 2. Seated Curls

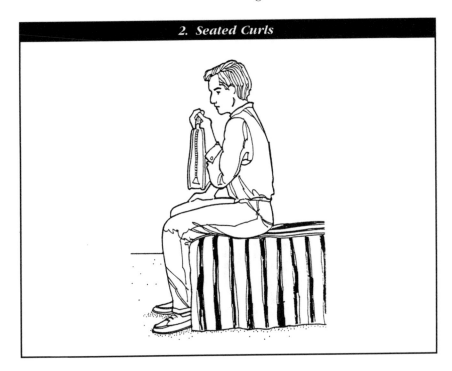

### 3. Bent Rows

Place your left knee and left arm on your bed or chair with your right foot on the floor. Keep your right knee slightly bent. Holding the briefcase in your right hand, allow your right arm to hang straight down. With your back straight, slowly raise the briefcase to your chest. Then lower. Repeat 8-20 times.

Repeat this exercise by placing your right knee and right arm on your bed or chair with your left foot on the floor. Holding the briefcase in your left hand, allow your left arm to hang straight down. Slowly pull the briefcase to your chest and then lower. Repeat 8-20 times. Again, be sure to keep your back straight through the move.

You can add to this workout by packing your favorite music and player; a stretch tape; light, portable weights; or exercise tubing. Exercise tubing, sold as the Sportscord, Traveling Trainer, BodyCord, or other brand names, can be used in lieu of weights or conventional exercise equipment to strengthen and stretch every muscle group in the body. Working like an industrial-strength rubber band, the tubing provides the exact amount of resistance desired. The great thing about exercise tubing is that it weighs almost nothing, fits into any suitcase,

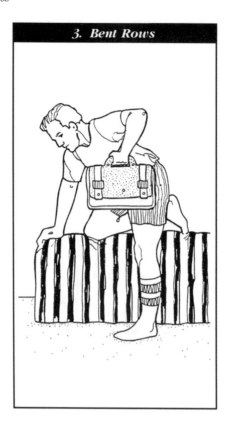

**3. Bent Rows**

and can be used anywhere. Most major sporting goods stores carry it. Examples of exercises that can be performed with exercise tubing usually come with the product. Or consider asking a trainer for personalized tips on how to use it.

Amenities found in almost any hotel room also can double as exercise equipment to add to your options. For example, Debbie Wloch, a Chicago-based traveler, uses phone books as arm weights to work her triceps and biceps and as a platform for calf raises. If you feel more comfortable following an exercise instructor, turn on your TV in the early morning. In most cities, a.m. programming includes exercise shows.

## Workout #3: The Pool Workout

Swimming after a long day on the road provides a superb aerobic workout while being gentle on your joints. It's a great break from the pounding of high-impact aerobics and running and also works your body's major muscle groups. "Swimming is one of the best exercises because the water provides a constant resistance throughout the entire strength curve," says Sean Morgan, personal trainer at Physis Prevention Center in San Francisco.

You don't have to be familiar with the conventional swim strokes—freestyle, butterfly, breaststroke, backstroke—to get quality exercise from a swimming pool. If you know how to dog paddle or tread water, you can get excellent exercise in just a few minutes—and keep your hair dry. Here are two water workouts you can do in any size hotel pool.

### 1. Speed Boating

Speed boating is basically the dog paddle stroke in high gear. Keeping your head out of the water, simply kick your legs as hard as you can. Keep your arms slightly bent while making a paddling or circular motion with your hands in front of your chest. Your arms and hands should not break the water's surface. This provides constant resistance throughout the movement. This added resistance creates a strenuous aerobic workout within seconds. Try to go as fast as you can in an aquatic sprint of 5-15 yards, stopping if you run out of breath. If the pool is longer than 15 yards, stop and rest along the side. Repeat 5-10 times depending on your fitness level.

**1. Speed Boating**

### 2. *Treading Water*

Most people may not view treading water as a real workout. But just 3-5 minutes of treading water provides great cardiovascular exercise. All you need is a pool that's at least four to five feet deep. The great advantage is that you don't have to swim around other bathers in a crowded pool. To tread water, simply remain in an upright position while moving your legs and feet under the water as if you were riding a bicycle. Move your hands and arms at the water's surface from the center of your chest to your sides. Keep repeating back and forth. Tread water for 3-5 minutes. Rest as needed. Repeat 2-3 times.

2. *Treading Water*

Other pool options if you're not a great swimmer include walking or running in the shallow end or using a kick board to do laps. Also many hotels and fitness clubs offer water aerobics classes.

## *Workout #4: The Walk That's More Than a Walk*

Walking is a great way to see an area and have fun while exercising at the same time. No matter what else comprises your travel fitness repertoire, walking should be a part of it. "It's a portable, convenient, user-friendly exercise. It's a universal activity that most people can do under most conditions," says James Gavin.

Here we suggest a circuit walk which incorporates stretching, strength training, and enhanced aerobic elements. First, chart a course which will take 35-40 minutes to complete. As alternatives to outdoor walking, consider a shopping mall or indoor running track. Once you've found a safe place to do the circuit walk, follow this sequence of exercises. If you're concerned with how far you've walked, wear a pedometer.

1. Walk at a slow, leisurely pace about 4-5 minutes.

2. First circuit break: Perform the no-time stretches outlined earlier in this chapter.

3. Walk at a moderate pace 4-5 minutes.

4. Second circuit break: Do 15-20 jumping jacks.

5. Walk at a brisk pace for 4-5 minutes.

6. Third circuit break: Find an object in the environment—a tree, mailbox, wall, or park bench—and do 15 to 20 standing push-ups. With feet spaced shoulder-width apart, stand at arms length from the object. Then, while keeping your body straight, bend your arms and lean toward the object. Push your body back to its original position. Next, do 10 to 15 squats as described in the Express Hotel Room Workout.

7. Walk at a moderate pace for 4-5 minutes.

8. Fourth circuit break: Repeat the no-time stretches.

9. Walk at a slow, leisurely pace for 4-5 minutes.

You can make this routine more strenuous by increasing walking time. Also consider interspersing different circuit break exercises. Gavin, for example, looks for opportunities in the environment to make a walk into a circuit. "If I'm in a park, I'll use a jungle gym or other things that I can exercise on," he says.

# Coping With an Unfamiliar Exercise Facility

Let's say you've decided to brave the hotel's gym or a nearby club. Being confronted with a roomful of unfamiliar exercise equipment can be an intimidating experience. "Many of my clients have walked into hotel gyms, looked around at the new equipment, and walked out because it looked too different," says Kim Chagwin, director of fitness at Physis Prevention Center in San Francisco.

If you stick around long enough to acquaint yourself with the equipment, however, you'll probably discover that it's not much different from what's in your gym at home. Most aerobic and cardiovascular equipment is pretty much standardized. If you've tackled stepping machines, stair climbers, or treadmills at home, you shouldn't have a problem with similar equipment on the road. Weight-training equipment doesn't vary that much either. Going from Universal to Cybex or Nautilus, for example, isn't going to make a big difference; you can *usually* do the same motions and work the same muscles on each. "The color, look, pins, and weights may be different, but the machine is actually the same," says Chagwin. But be wary of the weight settings. They don't equate. "A setting of 120 on one machine isn't 120 on the next," says Chagwin. It's best to start lighter than usual and work slowly up to a higher setting. Experts recommend starting at half your normal workload until you're used to the machine and then gradually increasing your resistance to meet your particular needs. "Don't take it for granted that you can do things the same way you do at home," Chagwin warns.

Be especially careful using new equipment which can place different stresses on different parts of your body. "Try to use the best possible technique because if you're not used to the equipment, you might injure yourself," says Dr. Gordon. If a machine is completely different from what you're used to, avoid it unless there's a trainer on staff who can help you.

Never hesitate to ask for help in a new health club. "It's like asking for directions when we're lost on the road—a lot of us don't want to do it," says Gavin, who has encountered too many reluctant travelers at his health club in the Westin Hotel in Montreal. Gavin recounts the story of one hotel guest who started a treadmill machine only to discover it was set way too fast for him. "He pressed the button and went flying on his behind," says Gavin. Above the machine was a big sign: DO NOT USE THIS MACHINE UNLESS YOU HAVE BEEN INSTRUCTED IN ITS PROPER USE. "People need to bite the bullet and just ask about the equipment," he says.

# Don't Forget Safety

Walking or jogging in an unfamiliar city is no time to be on automatic pilot. Staying alert and taking a few simple precautions are required when exercising outdoors away from home. One person we know learned this lesson the hard way. She was out jogging in a new town without I.D. on her. About a half mile from her hotel, she fell and sprained her ankle. Lying on the pavement in pain, she realized that she had no idea where she was. "I thought, if something happened to me, no one would know. It would take awhile for anyone to even identify me." Luckily she was assisted back to her hotel. Her experience exemplifies a key safety principle: Never embark on a jog or walk without knowing exactly where you're going and about how long you'll be gone. Ask the concierge or local residents for suggestions on safe routes and neighborhoods. Gravitate towards well-populated, well-lighted areas. Obtain a map of the area and plan your course. If possible, drive an unfamiliar exercise route before walking or running it. Before leaving, advise the concierge or a fellow traveler where you're headed and about how long you'll be gone.

While out, stay aware of your environment and make a mental note of landmarks to help find your way back. Run, walk, or bike with your head up to help stay aware of who and what is around you. Stay off the road if possible. Keep in mind that residents of different geographic areas vary in their familiarity and receptivity to outdoor athletes. In Portland, Oregon, a jogger has plenty of companions, and drivers expect his or her presence. In Savannah, Georgia, on the other hand, a jogger or fitness walker may startle a driver or two.

Always carry an I.D. and just enough cash to appease a mugger, to make a phone call, or to catch a cab if you lose your way, but don't carry or wear valuables. Wear white or reflective clothing at night. Tote mace, a whistle, or siren device. Take your room key with you or leave it at the desk. Consider leaving your Walkman at home. Listening to your favorite tunes, while a great cure for boredom, reduces your sensory awareness. Ideally, find someone to run or walk with. There really is safety in numbers.

# The International Workout

Too many of us succumb to the challenges of working out in another country and simply forgo exercise when traveling internationally. In a 1993 mail survey by *USA Today*, only 6% of respondents cited exercise as something they did during free time on international business trips. Says veteran traveler Jim Topinka, "Most American cities are pretty manageable, but when you go outside the United States, there's still a real question of how to work out." Alaskan physician Mark Beirne agrees. When he traveled to Ireland, he met the fitness challenge of his life. "They don't have fitness clubs there. I had to get out and walk and do calisthenics on my own," he says.

Cultural differences pose a key difficulty which must be addressed before exercising on foreign turf. "The American attitude towards exercise isn't universal," says James Gavin. While many Asian countries share our passion for state-of-the-art health clubs, many countries in Europe don't. Jogging on the streets of Shanghai may turn a few heads because the culture doesn't support that kind of activity. Jogging on a trip to Saudi Arabia during prayer time may incur the wrath of the police. Risk a few stares but never anything more serious—always check the local customs before embarking on any exercise program.

Cultural differences and limitations make it imperative to have a portable fitness routine when traveling abroad. Having various exercise options at your disposal, like the No-Time or Express Hotel Workouts outlined earlier in the chapter, give you the flexibility to work out anywhere. Not surprisingly the preferred exercise of most international travelers is walking or running because both are fairly easy to accomplish anywhere. You might add to that your own stretching or strength-training routines.

Creative globe trotters find a way to exercise while abroad no matter what. Gavin, for example, relies on tai chi movements which he has studied over the past 20 years and which can be done anywhere. One instructor informed him that the movements can even be performed in a phone booth; as of yet he hasn't had the need. One traveler told us she never goes to Europe without a mini step machine. She even steps on long train rides!

Performing a stretching or aerobic routine that you've practiced at home also helps in coping with the dissociation caused by international travel. "It's sort of a security blanket," says Gavin. "In a sense you feel at home once you settle into a familiar exercise program."

There are some sensible rules to follow while exercising, especially outdoors, in another country. If you're walking or jogging, try to blend in with the locals. In poor countries, don't jog in expensive or flashy clothes. Wearing designer sweats in the Third World is like having a placard on your back reading FOREIGNER. It might attract the wrong kind of attention. Also, make sure to follow the safety tips detailed in the preceding section. They're even more important to abide by on foreign turf.

Consider a jogging track at a local university rather than the roads of an unfamiliar place. Different driving habits of the locals, or cars on the "wrong side" of the road, can be disorienting, even dangerous. On his first trip from South Africa to the United States, Dr. Gordon learned this lesson the hard way. "I was at a convention in San Diego and went out for a jog. In the first five minutes, I nearly got run over three times. After that I just ran around one block so I wouldn't have to cross the road." We recommend facing the boredom of a running track rather than the perils of the street.

Pay attention also to environmental considerations at your destination and how they may affect your exercise. Differences in weather, air quality, altitude, and terrain must be factored into the fitness equation. Going for a strenuous run after arriving in Bogota, Colombia, 8,000 feet above sea level, for example, may leave you short of breath and disoriented, both symptoms of altitude sickness. Keep track of how these environmental elements affect the quality of your exercise. "Don't live in denial," says Gavin. "Some people want to believe the body is an infinitely adjustable entity and that it can take all kinds of stresses, so they fail to account for the changes in the environment."

When exercising in high altitudes or in hot, humid conditions, reduce the intensity and duration of your workout and give yourself plenty of time to acclimate. If you're in Mexico City or other polluted destinations where poor air quality will impair cardiovascular performance even in healthy individuals, opt to work out indoors if at all possible. Avoid exercising along a busy road or highway where pollution levels are higher. In one study, athletes had three times the concentration of harmful chemicals in their bloodstreams after running in a polluted city. The increase was equivalent to smoking ten to twenty cigarettes a day. Remember, air quality is best in the morning and after rush hour when ozone levels tend to be lower.

# The Travel Workout Checklist

Here are the main points for taking your workout on the road:

❑ Set your travel workout goals.

❑ Schedule regular on-the-road fitness appointments.

❑ Stay in a hotel with a fitness facility or access to a nearby club.

❑ Research fitness options at your destination.

❑ Listen to your body while exercising.

❑ Follow a balanced fitness program on the road.

❑ Get enough exercise to maintain your fitness level.

❑ Keep an open mind.

❑ At a minimum, accumulate at least 30 minutes of moderate-intensity physical activity on most days of your trip.

❑ Work out in the morning.

❑ Start with half your normal weight load on an unfamiliar exercise machine.

❑ Keep safety in mind.

# Avoiding Excess Baggage: How to Eat Right on Your Next Trip

*"I've run more risks eating my way across the country than in all my driving."*

Duncan Hines
*Adventures in Good Eating,* 1956

ike many travelers, Atlanta businessman Joe Rincon racked up the pounds along with his frequent-flier mileage. In four years of business travel, he put on 40 to 50 lbs. "When you're on the road, food becomes your friend," he said in an interview with *USA Today.* "You're very much alone, and you look forward to the next meal. During the day, you start thinking, 'What am I going to eat tonight?' Pretty soon, you start treating yourself to richer and richer foods."

Business travelers are notorious for abandoning their nutritional sense as soon as they leave their home kitchen. Travelers so often skip breakfast, dine on fast-food at lunchtime, and binge at dinner—depleting their health even more than their expense account. According to a recent survey, most of the top health ailments endured by travelers relate to diet, including upset stomachs, heartburn, indigestion, diarrhea, and constipation. Splurging during a once-a-year vacation never hurt anyone, but if you're eating a high-fat, high-cholesterol, high-calorie diet regularly on business trips, you're headed for health trouble. Based on our interviews with veteran travelers, here are some of the top reasons why diets take a major detour on the road:

- Emotional eating to reduce travel-induced feelings of stress, boredom, and anxiety;
- The loss of an at-home diet routine;
- Failure to plan ahead and set diet priorities;
- Adoption of a "vacation mentality," even on business trips, in which anything goes;
- The sheer number of opportunities to eat rich, non-nutritious foods;
- Social pressure from clients and colleagues to indulge;
- Time crunch that forces poor food choices;
- Lack of know-how to eat smart while dining out;
- Increased alcohol consumption; and
- Leaving your willpower at home.

Change can be as simple as identifying your on-the-road diet traps, learning to plan ahead, recognizing low-fat selections, and bolstering your travel willpower. Start now by rating your typical travel diet in the following quiz.

## Travel Diet Quiz

Take a few minutes to reflect on how you've eaten on your most recent trips. Then, circle "yes" or "no" in response to the following questions:

|  | Circle one | |
|---|---|---|
| 1. On the road, I find myself eating when I'm not hungry. | yes | no |
| 2. I'm so pressured and tightly scheduled on most trips that I eat whatever is available. | yes | no |
| 3. Oftentimes when I travel, I'll skip breakfast, grab a quick lunch, and splurge at dinner. | yes | no |
| 4. Sometimes when dining out for a business meal, I'll order a bottle of wine, desserts, or other rich foods to "set the right tone" for clients or colleagues. | yes | no |

5. If my flight is delayed, I typically find a place to eat or drink at the airport to pass time.     yes     no

6. I usually snack from the mini-bar in my hotel room.     yes     no

7. Sometimes on the road I will go for more than five hours without eating food.     yes     no

8. Occasionally I'll order special treats from room service because no one is there to see what I'm eating.     yes     no

9. I'll eat anything once to get a taste of the local or ethnic flavor of a city.     yes     no

10. When I eat out, I feel that I should eat everything on my plate.     yes     no

11. I never bring my own food with me when I travel.     yes     no

12. When the flight attendant shuttles down the aisle offering honeyed peanuts or other goodies, I have been unable to resist, even when I'm not hungry.     yes     no

13. I feel that my options are very limited for eating healthfully on the road.     yes     no

14. When away, I daydream and think about food more than I do at home.     yes     no

15. I eat fast food while traveling more than I do at home.     yes     no

16. I don't feel comfortable making special requests for low-fat dishes or other healthy choices at a restaurant, especially in front of business clients.     yes     no

17. I sometimes feel that "anything goes" with my diet when I travel because I'll get back on track when I get home.     yes     no

18. I drink more alcohol when I'm traveling.     yes     no

TOTAL    ___    ___

Responding "yes" to any one of these questions could spell diet disaster if you travel frequently. Tally your "yes" responses and rate your travel diet below.

Score

12-18     You're leaving your nutritional know-how at home. You need to incorporate new ways to eat healthy into your travel plans.

5-11     You're falling into many travel dietary traps. You need to make some changes to avoid trouble later on.

1-4     You're doing pretty well, but there's always room for improvement.

How did you score in the travel diet quiz? Did any statements seem particularly relevant to you? Consider keeping a travel diet diary on your next trip to pinpoint exactly where you're veering off-course. Just write down everything you put in your mouth during the trip, what the circumstances are, and how you're feeling. Once you've identified your weaknesses, prepare a strategy for how you'll cope next time you're on the road. Don't be discouraged if your waistline has been expanding as your travel increases. We'll show you some simple strategies for taking charge of your diet on the road.

# Plan Ahead

As travelers, we spend hours devising our itineraries and wrangling with travel agents, but don't give a minute to thinking about how we plan to eat while away. We usually depart thinking that we won't blow our diets this time. But once away from the routines of home, we invariably find ourselves inquiring about the double-chocolate decadence number on the dessert menu, gobbling the turn-down sweets, or raiding the mini-bar in the hotel room. What went wrong?

"Too few travelers have a diet plan for how they'll handle temptations and weaknesses on the road," says Carol Ceresa, M.H.S.L., R.D., chief clinical nutritionist at California Pacific Medical Center in San Francisco. "Travelers need to create a mindset where their health and nutritional status are priorities even though they're in a different environment. If they have a clear plan to follow, it's a lot easier to stick to than if they only have a vague idea of what they want to accomplish."

Ask yourself some key questions to help set your diet priorities for your next trip. Is this a short, once-a-year business trip where it won't matter much if you take a vacation from your normal diet? Or is this an extended trip, or one of many you take each year, making diet an important concern? Is your goal to maintain your pretrip weight, or do you have other special nutritional needs? Do you have health problems that make it critical to avoid salt, sugar, or fat? How important to your well-being is it to eat three meals on a regular schedule each day? Try to set one or two specific goals and commit them to writing before you leave. Be realistic. Attempting to replicate your at-home diet or to lose five pounds on your next trip only invites failure—and the self-loathing that follows. Aim to enjoy good food without injuring your health.

If you've identified recurring weaknesses, brainstorm ways to correct them without depriving yourself. For example, if you always order a bottle of wine over a business dinner, consider ordering one glass of chardonnay for yourself with mineral water on the side and alternate sips. That way, you invite clients and colleagues to partake, without burdening yourself with extra calories. Or, if you habitually overeat at business meals, where multi-course, caloric extravaganzas prevail, limit them to one a day. You might want to pack a fat gram, sodium, cholesterol, or calorie counter to help you meet your goals.

To translate your goals into concrete action, plan ahead. There are many creative ways to take charge of your travel diet before you leave home that don't take a lot of time or fancy planning. One simple predeparture strategy is to pack your own nutritious fare. Toss apples, oranges, low-fat whole wheat crackers, or other snacks into your briefcase or tote bag. If you'll be cruising the interstate, stuff an ice chest with nutritious snacks. "There's no excuse not to eat right in the car," says Elizabeth Somer, M.A., R.D., author of *Nutrition for Women: The Complete Guide* (1993). "You don't have to stop at every McDonald's and Burger King. If you do, get a McLean hamburger and ask them to hold the sauce, order orange juice, and supplement the meal with raw carrots and celery from the ice chest in the car." You can even freeze a sandwich ahead of time to keep it fresh en route.

Nutritious snacks between meals are a great way to avoid energy slumps in the mid-morning and afternoon. Some travelers even pack an immersion heater to warm instant soups and herbal teas. By packing snacks, you'll never be forced to go too long without food, encouraging a descent into primal junk-food foraging. If you miss your connection, you won't be at the mercy of the vendor selling diet-killer sticky buns in the terminal. And you just might be able to control at least one entire meal by eating it in your room.

Here are some healthful snacks that travel well:

- Bottled water
- Boxed juices
- Herbal teas
- Instant, dry soups
- Pop-top cans of tuna
- Fruit (fresh and dried)
- Raw vegetables
- Dry cereal/oatmeal packets

- Bagels
- Low-fat bran muffins
- Sports or energy bars
- Salt-free pretzels
- Low-fat crackers
- Fat-free tortilla chips
- Air-popped popcorn
- Raw bran and dried prunes
- Packages of ketchup, mustard, or jam
- Skim milk powder for your coffee or tea

Another way to take charge of your on-the-road diet is to always call ahead. If you know where you're going to eat, find out if they accept special orders. Will they make substitutions? Are there enough healthy options to choose among? If you're dining with others, suggest the restaurant yourself. Ask the concierge or a business contact to suggest a restaurant that serves pasta, fresh salads, vegetables, and other interesting low-fat, low-calorie food. If you're traveling by air, call in advance for one of those special meals we discussed in Chapter 2. Make sure to order what you really want. Don't assume that because you're requesting a vegetarian or low-cholesterol meal that it also will be low-fat, advises Somer. If you want a low-fat meal, ask for it.

As you plan your diet strategy, especially for an extended stay, try to limit your number of restaurant meals. Over many days, it's just too hard to eat every meal out without giving in to temptation. A realistic goal is to eat one meal a day in your room. This helps tremendously in gaining some control of the foods you're eating. Where you stay will influence your success. If you check into a Marriott Residence Inn with a kitchenette, for example, you'll have many more meal options than afforded by a standard hotel room. At the very least, angle for a room with a refrigerator. Also, call ahead to the concierge and ask about that much-overlooked traveler's friend: the grocery store. If you haven't packed nutritious fare, you can purchase healthful goodies at a nearby store or market. Many major food chains also offer sumptuous salad bars and prepared dinners.

# Five Principles of the Road Warrior's Core Diet

To keep your energy level high and your weight in check, keep these simple diet principles in mind when you travel.

## 1. Think Complex Carbohydrates

There's nothing obscure about a healthy on-the-road diet. Simply focus on obtaining 55 to 65 percent of your calories from complex carbohydrates. Choose a variety of fresh, minimally processed plant foods whenever possible. Seek out six servings a day of whole grain foods, breads, cereals, rice, and pasta, and five servings a day of fruits and vegetables. These foods won't make you fat and tend to curb cravings for diet-killer foods like potato chips and ice cream. If you work out on the road, eating foods rich in complex carbohydrates as soon as possible after you exercise offers the bonus of quickly restoring glycogen to your muscles and glucose to your bloodstream—so your body is ready to exercise again.

For protein, look for low-fat dairy products like non-fat yogurt or cottage cheese, fish, fowl, legumes, and beans. Eat small amounts of red meat, and limit your intake of salt, sugar, cholesterol, and caffeine.

## 2. Cut the Fat

"When you're on the road, it's easier to get a candy bar out of a vending machine than to find a grapefruit and peel it," says Judge Gary Schmidt. That simple reality probably explains why many traveler's core diets consist of fat. According to one survey, a whopping 45 to 48 percent of the total calories consumed by frequent business travelers come from fat, which is well above the 30 percent maximum fat allowance recommended by most experts.

"The hazards of the road are very real, with obesity being the main one," says Dr. John P. Foreyt, director of the Nutrition Research Clinic at Baylor College in Houston. "As a traveler, make sure you're paying attention to one thing, and one thing only, and that's fat grams."

Later on, we'll discuss tips for avoiding hidden fat traps while dining out.

## 3. Seek Fiber-Rich Foods

Getting enough fiber is never more important than when you're on the road. It not only relieves the major bane of travel—constipation—but also has been shown to lower blood cholesterol and reduce the risk of colon cancer. Great sources of dietary fiber include whole grain breads, high-fiber bran cereals, beans, oat bran, oatmeal, brown rice, dried prunes, and other fruits and vegetables. Bring along some raw bran in a container, and sprinkle it on your cereal or drink it in the morning with water.

## 4. Drink Plenty of Water

Whether you're shuttled in a bone-dry airplane or driving without access to fluids, travel is dehydrating. Never leave home without bottled water, and drink at least six to eight glasses a day to keep your body regular, hydrated, and energized.

## 5. Limit Your Alcohol

Watch your alcohol consumption. Alcohol is loaded with empty calories. While you won't accumulate fat grams by imbibing, studies show that the body burns fat less efficiently when alcohol is consumed. Alcohol plays another sinister role as a willpower destroyer. As one pithy traveler put it: "After one glass of wine, I'm two steps closer to having dessert."

# Don't Forget Breakfast

You know the set-up. You're not hungry in the morning when you travel. Or, maybe you're exhausted from the flight the night before and would rather sleep through breakfast.

We all find good-sounding excuses to explain why we don't eat breakfast on the road. According to one survey, 40 percent of business travelers skip breakfast on occasion. These are the folks nodding off during presentations, annoying others with their fuzzy-headed inquiries, sloshing coffee to keep their eyes open, or scarfing down donuts at mid-morning. Breakfast is even more important for those who have worked out first thing in the morning; they'll soon be running on empty without a solid meal.

To motivate yourself to eat breakfast, consider the following benefits of this often ignored meal:

• Breakfast boosts your blood sugar level to keep you mentally alert and physically energized throughout the day. With all the stresses of being on the road, you can't afford the added fatigue, irritability, and inability to concentrate caused by running on empty. What's more, if you don't refuel your energy stores in the morning, you can't make up for it later in the day, says Somer. "Even if you eat a good lunch, it never brings your energy level back up to the point it would have been if you had eaten breakfast."

• Breakfast helps you eat better throughout the day. You're less likely to be the victim of fat-laden snack attacks or late-in-the-day binge sessions if you eat breakfast. Scrimping on food early in the day virtually guarantees that you'll be flooding your body with excess calories at lunch or dinner. Such calorie loading "tends to overwhelm your body with calories that it does not need at that moment. And you know where the body puts the extra calories it doesn't need—in fat on the waist, hips, thighs, and so forth," writes Evelyn Tribole, in her book *Eating on the Run.*

• Breakfast helps you meet your weight-control goals. Meal skippers have a lower metabolism, which makes it harder for them to lose weight, says Tribole. Eating breakfast helps the body burn more calories in the morning and throughout the day. Research at Vanderbilt University has shown that overweight women who ate breakfast lost slightly more weight than those who didn't. There's even evidence that breakfast eaters have lower cholesterol levels than those who skip it.

Maybe now you're convinced of the merits of breakfast. But what should you order? Great choices for breakfast on the road include oatmeal or a multi-grain cereal with skim milk, fruit, and orange juice; french toast made with egg whites only; a dry bagel, toast, or a low-fat muffin with jam; non-fat yogurt or low-fat cottage cheese, and fruit; an egg-white omelet; pancakes with a fruit or yogurt topping (hold the butter); even a banana with a glass of skim milk. Those all-you-can-eat, all-American breakfast buffets in the hotel restaurant can get you off to a good start, provided you make the right selections. Just avoid those croissants and pats of butter.

If nothing looks healthy on the menu or at the buffet, ask the server to check in the kitchen for dry cereals, low-fat milk, or other heart-friendly staples. With a little ingenuity, you should be able to find something healthy to eat for breakfast. Even McDonald's offers pancakes and fat-free apple-bran muffins.

Or, handle breakfast in your room, especially if you're crunched for time. How long does it take to order skim milk and coffee from room service and supplement it with the dry cereal, fruit, or crackers you packed with you or purchased from a local store? Or to buy your own low-fat milk, juice, and yogurt in advance and put it in your mini-refrigerator or a bucket with ice in your room? You might even eat leftover pizza or other doggie-bag goodies from the night before. Some travelers have a meal-replacement powder drink in the morning, even if they're not dieting. It's not ideal, but it's better than nothing. Do something—anything—to jump start your engine in the morning.

# Four Strategies for Eating Smart When Dining Out

Whether you're grabbing a bite at an airport eatery, a roadside restaurant, or a high-priced in-city spot, there are some basic strategies for healthy dining during those inevitable meals out. The goal is to make smart selections without compromising taste. It doesn't make sense to eat something you don't like just because it's good for you. After all, food is something to be *enjoyed*. There's no need for self-deprivation, just smart choices. So many restaurants now offer delectable low-fat entrees. Would you really feel cheated ordering broiled chicken with apples and shallots, grilled swordfish in a vinaigrette, or other low-fat entrees? Airports even offer interesting, healthful selections. At San Francisco International Airport, you can get sushi. Eating out need not spell diet disaster. Here are four easy tips for smart restaurant eating without feeling deprived.

## 1. Order With the Road Warrior's Core Diet in Mind

Keep those simple, healthy diet principles discussed on pages 141 and 142 in mind when you study the menu. Look for carbohydrate- and fiber-loaded pastas, vegetables, and salads. If these healthy options aren't on the menu, ask the waiter what the chef can whip up or find another restaurant.

## 2. Recognize Healthy, Low-Fat Selections

Many healthy-sounding foods are really fat traps for the unwary. A trip to the salad bar, for instance, can be a diet saver, but not if you pile on croutons, bacon bits, and grated cheese. You need to become a culinary detective of sorts and read between the lines of the restaurant menu, uncovering hidden fat grams. There are some obvious places to start. Watch for heavy cheese or meat sauces and gravies—they're usually loaded with fat. According to a recent survey by the Center for Science in the Public Interest, an average restaurant serving of fettucine alfredo has 97 grams of fat, as much as in five McDonald's Quarter Pounders, whereas pasta with a tomato sauce has only 17 grams of fat—and the difference is entirely in the sauce. Avoid hollandaise, mayonnaise, and tartar sauces. Instead, look for sauces reduced from vegetables. At the very least, always request the sauce on the side so you can limit how much you use.

Order your salad dressing on the side as well. As a rule of thumb, one tablespoon of salad dressing contains a whopping 100 calories.

Try diluting your favorite dressing with balsamic vinegar or lemon juice, or switch to a low-fat option. Keep the butter and olive oil off of your bread. You might try non-fat yogurt, low-fat sour cream, or just red and black pepper on your baked potato. Remember that cream or butter might be hidden in anything stuffed, mashed, or whipped; one or the other may also be lurking in your soup. Order a vegetable-based soup thickened with rice, not cream. Avoid meat-based soups, which are high in fat.

What are some healthy meal orders? For lunch sandwiches, stick with chicken, turkey, or tuna, piled with vegetables on a whole grain bread. Broiled or grilled seafood of any kind with steamed vegetables is a good bet. Baked chicken is fine; just take the skin off, and eat only the white meat. Skinless dark meat has more than twice the fat, 20 percent more calories, and 10 percent less protein than white meat. If you're at a banquet where everyone gets the same thing, cut or scrape off any fried topping or fat. Pasta is great; just remember to choose a tomato-based sauce. Good dessert choices include fresh berries, fruit sorbet, or non-fat frozen yogurt.

Knowing how to read between the lines on any menu is key to making a healthy selection. The table below lists common menu red flags and menu buzz words to look for.

## 3. Ask, Ask, Ask!

If there's one rule to remember when dining out, it's be assertive when ordering. "And that includes finding out what is in the food

### Fat Watchers' Red Flags and Buzz Words

| Red flags (high-fat) | Buzz words (low-fat) |
|---|---|
| Battered | Baked |
| Crisp | Charbroiled |
| Fried | Roasted |
| Sauteed | Grilled |
| Au gratin | Steamed |
| Pastry-wrapped | Broiled |
| Basted | Poached |
| Buttered | Boiled |
| Creamed | Stir-fried |
| Scalloped | Marinara/tomato sauce |
| Breaded | Light wine sauce |

you're eating and dealing with peer pressure when everyone else is ordering high-fat junk," says Dr. Foreyt. "It's amazing that someone would let the person sitting next to them dictate what they're going to order."

Enlist the server as your dietary ally. Ask how the food is prepared. Make sure that it meets your special dietary needs and doesn't contain excess or hidden fat. If an entree is described as low-sodium, low-cholesterol, or low-fat, what's been added as a substitute? Never assume anything. The menu may say an item is low in cholesterol, but it may be loaded with oil, says Helen Rasmussen, M.S., R.D., with the Human Nutrition Research Center at Tufts University. "Keep in mind you're the customer—and just ask," she says.

Feel free to make special requests or ask for substitutions. According to the National Restaurant Association, three out of four restaurants will alter how food is prepared if requested. If nothing looks healthy on the menu, ask the chef to prepare you a special pasta or vegetable dish. Many selections would be healthy if prepared a little differently. Could the entree be prepared with one-half the amount of salt or fat? Could the chef prepare a special low-fat sauce for the fish, instead of the advertised butter sauce? What about having the chicken steamed, broiled dry, or poached in white wine? Could skim milk be substituted for whole? Would the chef cut back on cheese and eggs? Could a baked potato or steamed vegetables be substituted for the french fries? But if those steamed vegetables arrive swimming in butter, send them back.

## 4. Exercise Creative Portion Control

With so many enticing options on most menus, many travelers are tempted to order "one of everything," especially if they arrive at their destinations half-starved. Try to keep in mind the amount of food you usually eat at home and keep to those approximate portions on the road. Remember, restaurants serve the same size meal, whether you're a 5-foot-2, 110-pound woman or a 6-foot-3, 220-pound star wrestler. Here are some tips from frequent travelers for keeping portions under control:

- Make healthy selections at all-you-can-eat buffets and smorgasbords, and decline a second trip to the buffet.

- Order without looking at the menu. Arrive at the restaurant with a healthy meal in mind, like steamed vegetables or broiled chicken, and just order it.

- Ask that the bread, butter, and anything else you don't want be taken off the table. You can easily consume hundreds of calories eating bread and butter before your appetizer or meal arrives. At home, do you sit around chewing on bread dipped in olive oil for 15 to 20 minutes before eating?

- Think substitutes. If you must have dessert, why not one cookie instead of a piece of pecan pie?

- Order a la carte. It makes it easier to control what you eat by limiting high-calorie side dishes.

- Order one or two appetizers as an entree with a dinner salad or light soup.

- Split one entree with a dining companion and order a salad on the side.

- Order lunch-sized portions at dinner.

- Finish your meal before ordering dessert.

- Don't feel obligated to clean your plate. Just because the food costs money doesn't mean you have to eat it all. Place a value on your health, and leave some food on your plate, or take it back to your room.

- If you're at a party or function, grab a sparkling water first, then possibly a glass of wine; never stand near the food buffet.

## Dine Safely While Abroad

Are you the type of intrepid traveler who can't wait to try the indigenous food of the new country you're visiting?

"People will travel to a place like Bolivia and see chiappas cooking on the side of the road and grab one," says Gary Schumacher, vice president of World Travel Partners in Atlanta. "The problem is that they're used to eating pre-digested hamburgers and this thing goes down like a brillo pad. It will wreak havoc with them for the rest of the trip."

Half the fun of international travel is getting a taste of the local color. But there are some simple, sensible precautions to avoid indigestion, traveler's diarrhea, and even worse fates. Once you leave the United States, Europe, Australia, and Canada, watch what you eat. There are plenty of microbes, parasites, bacteria, and other treacherous organisms in the cuisines of less-developed countries just waiting to tangle with your digestive tract.

# KNOW YOUR FAST-FOOD OPTIONS

Because of their convenience and reliability, fast-food restaurants are a staple of many travelers. In recent surveys of frequent travelers, 91 percent responded that at airports they were more likely to eat fast food than a full meal, and 25 percent admitted to dining on fast food at lunch time. To accommodate the throngs of hungry travelers, fast-food restaurants are popping up in airports, hotels, and roadsides around the world. If McDonald's is one of your on-the-road food groups, how can you survive with your arteries intact? Answer: order selectively, using the many strategies outlined in this chapter.

Luckily, there are more healthy selections than ever as more chains offer salads, lean burgers, and low-fat shakes. Many have switched from beef to vegetable fat for all frying. But not surprisingly, many choices continue to be nutritional nightmares, from Carl Jr.'s 1,030-calorie Double Western Bacon Cheeseburger to Jack in the Box's Ultimate Cheeseburger drenched in 16 teaspoons of fat. Few fast foods offer fewer than 30 percent of their calories from fat, writes Michael F. Jacobson, Ph.D, in his book, *Fast-Food Guide* (1991). Many fast foods are in the 40 to 50 percent fat range, with some even higher. "That's because the food that isn't high in fat to begin with gets dunked in fat before it's sold," he says. Order with care.

Virtually every fast-food chain offers nutritional information. If you're in doubt about what to order, ask to see the numbers. Or, use the fast-food scorecard in the table on p. 150. The scores were created by nutritionists at the Center for Science in the Public Interest by awarding points for vitamins, minerals, complex carbohydrates, and fiber, and subtracting points for fat, cholesterol, sodium, and other nutritional "no-nos." Choose foods with the highest scores and stay away from those near the bottom of the scorecard.

Start by choosing your restaurant with care. If you just landed in Coban, Guatemala, don't ask the airport cab driver to recommend a good dinner place. You might find yourself at his brother's hole-in-the-wall diner munching rancid corn tamales. A better bet is to ask your local business contacts or the hotel concierge for a good place to dine, says Schumacher.

Do some homework before you leave home. Many travel agents can access information on quality restaurants in any major city in the world. Certain travel guides, like the Lonely Planet series, also offer reliable advice on out-of-the-way eateries.

When you walk into a restaurant, be on guard for good hygiene. Before sitting down, head for the restroom and check its condition. Is there soap and running water? A means to dry your hands? If not, find another place to eat. Similarly, if you see other red flags—the silverware isn't clean, the chef is toothless and spitting tobacco, the serving staff doesn't look well-groomed, no one else is dining there—don't eat there, no matter how much you want the excitement of local food.

While in less developed countries, pay attention to what you put in your mouth. There's no rule requiring you to eat whatever the locals are eating—especially if it's iguana, dog, or cobra meat—to get the sales contract signed. Partake if you will, but keep your stomach and any special dietary needs in mind. Whatever you do, never fall prey to the tempting aromas wafting from the local street vendors. Those foods are extremely high-risk. Just how risky was exemplified in a recent Mexican Health Ministry study showing that no less than 80 percent of the food served on the streets of Mexico City contained fecal bacteria.

Follow this simple adage: "Boil it, cook it, peel it, or forget it." To avoid becoming ill from food grown in manure-enriched soil and washed in dirty water (common practices in many parts of the world), stay away from fresh salads and raw vegetables. Don't let your guard down even at major hotels. Only eat vegetables that have been cooked and are still hot. If you crave fruits and raw vegetables, only eat them if you washed and peeled them yourself first.

All meats and fish should be well-cooked and hot when they arrive at your table. If it's pink or lukewarm, send it back. Remember, if it's highly seasoned, it might be spoiled food in disguise. Avoid sausage and shellfish. Never eat raw meat, fish, or eggs (which may be lurking in your Caesar salad and other dishes). Use only commercial dairy products, including pasteurized milk, cheese, yogurt, and cottage

## Fast-Food Scorecard

| Food | Score |
| --- | --- |
| Wendy's baked potato, plain | 86 |
| Wendy's baked potato with broccoli and cheese | 41 |
| Taco Bell's bean burrito | 37 |
| McDonald's vanilla shake | 32 |
| McDonald's fat-free apple-bran muffin | 31 |
| Domino's 16-inch cheese pizza (2 slices) | 29 |
| Wendy's chili | 27 |
| Subway's turkey sub (6-inch) | 25 |
| McDonald's hot cakes with margarine and syrup | 21 |
| McDonald's McLean Deluxe | 9 |
| Pizza Hut's medium supreme pan pizza (2 slices) | 7 |
| Burger King's BK Broiler chicken sandwich | 1 |
| Domino's 16-inch pepperoni pizza (2 slices) | −2 |
| McDonald's french fries (medium) | −13 |
| Hardee's vanilla shake | −15 |
| Arby's roast beef sandwich | −27 |
| Taco Bell's beef taco | −28 |
| McDonald's Filet-O-Fish | −33 |
| McDonald's Egg McMuffin | −34 |
| Burger King's blueberry mini-muffins | −43 |
| Wendy's Big Classic | −48 |
| McDonald's Chicken McNuggets | −50 |
| McDonald's Big Mac | −51 |
| McDonald's apple pie | −56 |
| KFC Original Recipe, breast | −59 |
| Burger King french toast sticks | −68 |
| Burger King Croissan'wich with bacon, egg, and cheese | −117 |
| KFC Extra Crispy thigh | −121 |
| McDonald's sausage and egg biscuit | −144 |
| Burger King Double Whopper with cheese | −195 |

*Note.* Adapted from the Nutrition Scoreboard Poster, available (for $5) from the Center for Science in the Public Interest, 1875 Connecticut Ave. N.W., #300, Washington, DC, 20009-5728. Copyright 1992 by CSPI.

cheese. Stay away from food that has been sitting at room temperature or out in the sun, especially if it has mayonnaise in it.

Stick with chlorinated, boiled, or bottled water. This includes ice cubes and the water you brush your teeth with. According to the Centers for Disease Control, only boiled water; carbonated beverages, including carbonated bottled water and soft drinks; and beer and wine may be safe to drink in areas where sanitation is particularly poor.

## Building Your On-the-Road Willpower

Now that you've decided to take charge of your dietary destiny on your next trip and have the knowledge to do it, what's to stop you from eating right?

Answer: Those under-acknowledged, often intense feelings that travel creates. The biggest threat to your on-the-road willpower is your untamed feelings, which, if left unmanaged, just might compel you toward the ice cream stand or vending machine.

Let's say you're luggage is heading to Deadwood, South Dakota, without you. You're mad. Your plane was delayed three hours. You're bored. You'll be sleeping in a strange bed. You're anxious. You've been up all night on a red-eye and have a key speech to give two hours after arrival. You're overwhelmed. Certainly, a little chocolate bar would perk you up. What about a quick pass through the drive-through window for a vanilla shake? After all, you'll whip your diet back in shape when you get home. Get the picture?

Getting a grip on your travel-induced feelings will allow your will-power to emerge. If you find your willpower falling victim to travel anxiety and stress, the next chapter is for you. The smart traveler also saves his or her willpower stores by avoiding unnecessary temptations. You don't have to make your journey unreasonably difficult by showing that you can resist even the most delectable dietary enticements. Remove temptations whenever you can. At one Seattle-area hotel, guests are encouraged to "raid the pantry" after 11 p.m. Everything from cookies, pastries, and breads to lunch meats, gourmet mustard, and cheeses are left out in the open kitchen for guests with the late-night munchies. Presented with such an opportunity, you might head to the pantry, rationalizing that you'll only snatch an apple. More likely, you'll take some chocolate chip cookies back to your room as well. It's better to simply decline such invitations. You might also request fruit instead of sweets for your turn-down snack. Refuse the key to your mini-bar. To avoid feeling deprived, stash healthy snacks in your room instead. If you're a closet eater, don't even look at the room service menu. Do you really have to meet a client in the hotel lounge where there's enough free happy-hour hors d'oeuvres to feed an army? Why not suggest a walk through the city or a tennis match instead? Staying active will help keep the excess weight off.

If, despite your best intentions, your diet goals elude you today, don't throw in the towel for the rest of the trip. You'll get another chance tomorrow.

# The Eating Right Checklist

Next time you're struggling with your diet on the road, keep these pointers in mind:

❏ Set your diet priorities before leaving.

❏ Pack some of your own food.

❏ Choose restaurants that serve healthy fare.

❏ Order foods rich in complex carbohydrates and fiber and low in fat.

❏ Make special requests for substitutions and healthy food preparation when necessary.

❏ Find the healthy selections at fast-food restaurants.

❏ Exercise portion control.

❏ Drink plenty of water.

❏ Limit alcohol.

❏ Never skip breakfast.

❏ Don't overlook the grocery store.

❏ On extended stays, try to eat one meal a day in your room.

❏ While dining abroad, boil it, cook it, peel it, or forget it.

❏ Manage your travel stress.

❏ Exercise.

❏ Avoid unnecessary temptations.

# *Managing Your Travel Stress*

It starts like this: You get the last-minute call to make the presentation at the branch office. Your flight leaves at 4:30 p.m. and you start packing at 3 p.m. You feel your body tense and your breathing quicken as you race against the clock, tossing essentials into your carry-on bag. By 3:30 p.m., you're in a full sweat and your stomach is in knots as you call a cab. You dash to the airport, barely making your flight. You board the plane, feeling limp and exhausted.

You've just experienced the stress-induced "fight-or-flight" response, the traveling companion of many executives. "When we are faced with situations that require adjustment of our behavior, an involuntary response increases our blood pressure, heart rate, rate of breathing, blood flow to muscles, and metabolism, preparing us for conflict or escape," writes Dr. Herbert Benson in his landmark book *The Relaxation Response* (1975). When the stress bell sounds, our bodies prime us to fight or flee. This came in handy for our ancestors who needed the adrenaline boost to occasionally battle a prehistoric predator, but for a Type-A executive on the road, the chronic elicitation of the fight-or-flight response can lead to hypertension, heart disease, and other problems. All those periods of travel-induced anxiety, frustration, and anger take their toll.

Dr. Benson defines stress as "environmental conditions that require behavioral adjustment." With this definition in mind, it's easy to see why travel, especially on business, can be a dramatic stress inducer. At every turn, travel confronts us with change. The traveler is transported to a new locale where he or she must confront the unknown and unfamiliar. Different surroundings, the absence of family and friends, possibly a new language, unfamiliar foods and customs—even a new bed—all require emotional and behavioral adjustment. Add to that the pressure of doing business on a tight schedule and you have a sure-fire recipe for stress. A 1988 study of business travelers by Hyatt Hotels & Resorts describes business travel as "a heightened, charged experience in which every pitfall is magnified, and every small inconvenience is perceived as a threat—not just to the business at hand, but also to the traveler's sense of personal mastery." While no two travelers will respond to the stress of the road in the same way, we can all expect to experience a little insecurity while traveling.

Despite the security concerns and uncertainty, the separation from family and friends, the traffic jams, the overbooked planes, the missed connections, the lost luggage, and the sometimes poor service from hotels and car rental companies, travel stress can be successfully managed. Henry David Thoreau once wrote, "The greatest art is to change the quality of the day." How are you at changing the quality of your travel day? Take the following **Travel Stress Quiz** to rate how you're coping.

# Travel Stress Quiz

Rate the level of your own travel stress. Circle "yes" or "no" next to each statement. Then add up the number of "yes" responses and interpret your score on the next page.

<u>Circle one</u>

1. I often feel tense, pressured, overloaded, overwhelmed, or hassled while traveling.　　　　yes　　no

2. My health, mood, appetite, sleep, or sex patterns have changed since being on the road.　　　　yes　　no

3. I feel that I've "paid my dues" with my company and that I shouldn't have to travel so much anymore.　　yes　　no

4. When something goes wrong, even little things, I often become irritable or lose my temper.　　yes　　no

5. I sometimes feel that my sense of control is threatened in one way or another on a trip.　　yes　　no

6. I drink more on the road just to calm down.　　yes　　no

7. On occasion, I've awakened in my hotel room and not known what city I was in.　　yes　　no

8. I often feel guilty leaving my family behind.　　yes　　no

9. I have little, if any, control over when and where I travel.　　yes　　no

10. Before leaving on a trip, I sometimes experience a sense of dread.　　yes　　no

11. When I have an unexpected block of free time because of a meeting cancellation or schedule change, I feel panicky.　　yes　　no

12. My performance at work has suffered recently.　　yes　　no

13. Travel often interferes with my family obligations and personal needs.　　yes　　no

14. I find it difficult to maintain or fear losing relationships because I'm gone so much.　　yes　　no

15. I worry often about my personal safety on the road.　　yes　　no

16. When I'm on the road, my days away are fully scheduled, leaving me with virtually no personal time.　　yes　　no

17. I wish things would go my way more often when  yes    no
    I'm on the road.

18. It's becoming more difficult to get back into my family  yes    no
    life after a trip.

TOTAL ___  ___

A "yes" response to any one question should alert you that you
may be experiencing the effects of travel stress. Tally up your "yes"
responses and see how you're coping with stress on the road.

Score

12-18   Your travel stress is getting the better of you. You need to
        implement some effective coping measures.

6-11    You may not be perceiving or handling stressors while travel-
        ing as well as you could be. Start now to change how you
        respond to the rigors of the road.

1-5     You're handling the unavoidable stress of travel fairly well.
        Set out to do it even better.

Because our experience of stress is integrally related to our overall
well-being, pay attention to the tips and strategies on diet, jet lag,
exercise, and more, outlined in the chapters of *Travel Fitness*. Here
we will investigate key behavioral and emotional changes you can
make to beat travel stress. We'll tell you how to:

- Recognize your own signs of travel stress,
- Regain control while on the road,
- Adopt a positive attitude towards travel,
- Prepare to beat stress,
- Pace yourself,
- Keep a routine,
- Create time for yourself,
- Find social support while away,
- Take care of your relationships while traveling, and
- Know what to do when travel stress strikes.

# Gaining Control

Experts say our biggest stressors are those events that threaten our sense of control or personal power. It's not the amount of stress posed by a given situation while traveling that determines an individual's response so much as the actual or perceived ability of the traveler to control the circumstances creating it. That's why an unexpected cancellation of a critical flight usually will stress a traveler more than missing a flight because of leaving too late for the airport. Both events are unpleasant but in the former case, the stress was created by a circumstance over which the traveler had no control—the airline's unpredictable scheduling—while the latter mishap could have been avoided had the traveler planned better. There's nothing worse than having something "just happen to you," despite your best efforts.

The travelers we interviewed who dealt best with the frustrations of the road took charge of as many aspects of their trip as possible. Obviously, there are events over which the traveler has absolutely no control. Long lines at the rental car counter, an auto that overheats on the freeway, or snarled traffic are some examples. Yet even over these seemingly uncontrollable events, the stress-resistant traveler seeks to gain what we call "secondary (or back-up) control." For example, if canceled flights have caused problems in the past, they will have their travel agent or corporate travel department prepare a list of alternative flights leaving within an hour of a scheduled departure. If a flight is canceled, instead of scrambling to find a new airline, they know where to go and how long they have to wait. Similarly, if they don't have time to wait for luggage, they only take carry-on bags. In the above examples, these travelers haven't controlled the occurrence or nonoccurrence of the negative event (canceled flight or delayed luggage), but they are ready to efficiently cope when disaster strikes. By anticipating and preparing for negative events outside their control, they've gained secondary or back-up control, which helps to minimize travel stress.

To gain your sense of control, take the time to create a two-column list of your on-the-road stressors, advises Dr. Paul Rosch, president of the American Institute of Stress and professor of medicine and psychiatry at New York Medical College. In one column list the travel stressors which you can control. This list might include such things as tight scheduling, social isolation, diet, or last-minute packing. Be as inclusive as possible, and consider opportunities to exercise secondary control. In the other, list those events over which you have no control.

Then, prioritize those things over which you have some control, and use your energy solving those travel problems instead of mentally agitating about things over which you have no control.

The simple act of concretely writing down and distinguishing between your travel stressors can help alleviate stress. "There are certain stresses in life that you can do something about and others you can't," says Dr. Rosch. "The wisdom is in being able to distinguish between the two, so that you're not constantly frustrated like Don Quixote tilting at windmills trying to change things that you can't hope to alter." Instead, devote your time and talents to areas where you can make a difference.

# The Importance of Attitude

Why is it that two travelers confronted with the same event can have two entirely different responses? Traveler A, when informed of a one-hour flight delay, focuses on the opportunity to read a long-neglected report; Traveler B gets into a screaming match with the airline personnel. The reaction to stress is highly individual. Whether due to temperament, genes, or learned coping style, one traveler's stress can be another's enjoyment.

We can change how we register and cope with travel stressors to improve the quality of a trip. Even if you can't control a given event, you can control your reaction to it. You also can control your overall outlook towards travel. For every negative of travel, there's at least one corresponding positive. Rekindle your sense of adventure. What does your trip give you an opportunity to do that you otherwise wouldn't do? Let's face it, even business travel gives you a break from humdrum routine. You're exposed to new people, cultures, foods, customs. You get a break from family responsibilities. You gain the heady sense of importance whisking off on a jet to conduct business on foreign turf. Maybe it's worth putting up with a few reservation errors or rocky flights to gain the many pluses of travel. Says veteran traveler Adam Taylor, a product manager at Microsoft in Redmond, Washington: "Travel is a state of mind. If you expect to be exhausted and to have mishaps, you're probably more likely to feel the effects of it."

One way to change your attitude on travel is to take a look at your underlying expectations which can be unrealistic, especially if you're a Type A personality, says Dr. Eric Goldstein, Ph.D., a psychologist and stress-management expert. "Watch out for the 'should' word," he

## TRAVEL FITNESS TIPS: WHITE-KNUCKLE FLIERS

You've seen them on the plane, gripping their hand rests, making the sign of the cross before takeoff, demanding cocktails on morning flights, anxiously studying the faces of crew members for signs of impending disaster. They are normally sensible individuals overcome by a fear of flying. From 25 to 30 million American adults are either anxious, fearful, or phobic of flying. It doesn't just strike novices; veteran business travelers, even long-time flight attendants, have succumbed to the fear. One businessman was so afraid his boss would ask him to fly that he started his own business. Another woman jetted on business from her Florida home to cities around the United States without a shudder until a plane she was on hit severe turbulence—and left her with a full-blown phobia. When asked to travel on business again, she resigned.

According to psychologists, the typical fearful flier tends to be a nervous type prone to perfectionism and a desire for control. They're emotional but less comfortable showing it than most. They also have great imaginations. With the first sign of turbulence, they're already envisioning the plane going down in flames. The phobia is often triggered during a turning point in life and may have nothing to do with flying itself, says Fran Grant, a pilot and cofounder of the Fear of Flying Clinic at San Francisco International Airport. Flying becomes the magnet on which the anxiety in a person's life collects.

If you suffer jangled nerves while flying, there's hope. With a little effort, fear of flying can be managed. The first step is to keep flying, no matter what. Because avoidance only feeds a phobia, if you stop or limit your flying, your fear will grow. You may end up grounded, along with your career.

When en route, challenge the alarmist thoughts crossing your mind. If the plane hits a pocket of turbulence in midflight, and you imagine a crash, ask yourself, Is what I'm saying true? Of course not! The cruising phase of a flight is the safest time of all, and planes are equipped to handle turbulence. "Think of the plane like a ship," says Grant. "The turbulence can rock you to sleep." Some fearful fliers snap a rubber band on their wrist to break negative thought patterns.

Knowing something about flying statistics, the basic mechanics of airplane flight, and the logistics of the air-traffic control network also can help. If you know why an airplane makes the sounds it does, you can recognize "friendly noises" and relax. It's also comforting to know that for every hour in the air, most planes spend five hours on the ground being serviced. Being a pilot isn't even viewed as a hazardous occupation by the insurance industry. In fact, by most accounts, your odds of a safe flight are 99.99998 percent.

OK, so you still have the jitters even after trying to reason yourself out of it. Accept it. Tell the crew that you're petrified to fly, and introduce yourself to the pilot. There's no reason to be embarrassed; after all, you're only one of millions who feel the same way. You'll feel a lot better sharing your fear than gripping your chair in silence.

To keep your anxiety at bay, distract yourself. Talk to your neighbor, listen to a relaxation tape, or read a good novel. Grant suggests planning what you will do every hour of the flight. Some flight attendants seat the fearful next to families with young children to ensure distraction. The goal is to stay focused on the present, thereby keeping your mind from worry. If you're suddenly gripped by fear, breath deeply. Try to relax the muscles in your body. If at all possible, don't suppress your fear with alcohol or medications. The resulting feelings of disorientation can actually worsen your phobia.

Try to be as relaxed as possible when you board the plane, says Grant. Avoid any food or beverages containing caffeine or sugar, which will only exaggerate your anxiety. Grant also recommends eating a diet rich in carbohydrates before and during your trip because of the relaxing effect on the body. A preflight workout also can help keep anxiety in check. Schedule a morning flight to avoid tension from mounting all day long. No matter what, don't rush getting to the airport.

If your self-help measures fail, you need not continue flying in a state of fright. Confront your fear head-on by attending one of the many programs devoted to helping people overcome aviophobia. USAir's five-week Fearful Flyers Program, (412) 366-8112, offered in 12 cities each year, is typical. The program combines group support, behavior modification techniques, and aviation education to help fliers deal with their fears. Participants, armed with relaxation tapes, brave a one-hour flight during the last session. About 97 percent of participants say they're flying much more comfortably after the program, says program director Carol Stauffer. Contact your local airport or travel agent to find out what is available near you. Some clinical psychologists also provide help to aviophobics.

advises. "I hear a lot of business executives say, 'The airlines *should* be able to leave on time.' But once you use the word 'should,' you're creating unrealistic expectations. Sure, it would be nice if flights ran on time, but having that expectation is probably not realistic."

Dr. Goldstein advises Type A travelers to abandon their competitive, perfectionist, and time-focused personalities—at least when they're on the road. "They need to learn the more easygoing Type B characteristics, and if they can't actually be those things, playact them when they're traveling," he says. "They need to see that all those demands aren't going to get their plane to leave on time."

Many travelers resist being on the road because they expected to stop traveling long ago or don't like their jobs. Their internal conflict about travel makes it tougher to cope with the rigors of the road. Were you told you could stop or cut back on travel, but now the current work environment won't allow it? Do you feel you've "paid your dues" and now resent each new travel assignment? If so, find some way to work through your feelings of conflict and unsatisfied expectations to improve your attitude towards travel. State your needs to management and brainstorm ways to cut back on travel and still keep your job.

## Prepare to Beat Stress

Nothing will help you manage travel stress more than superb preparation. The more planning you do before leaving, the less anxious you'll feel on the road. Preparation helps foster that sense of control so critical to reducing stress. One word of caution, however: Try to use your well-laid plans as a flexible guide, not as rules written in stone. Remember that any successful trip is a combination of planning and spontaneity.

To be better prepared, think of pretrip time-savers to help your transition into travel. You might develop a list of essentials to pack, such as extra medication, workout gear, a business planner, a folder for expenses, or your laptop computer (using a laptop with a built-in modem is a great way to send e-mail messages to co-workers back home without playing time zone phone tag). Consult the list before every trip. Consider creating a pocket-size reminder card listing important numbers that you always take with you. The card might include numbers for your corporate travel department or travel agent, business contacts, or frequent-flier identification. That way, if you're sent on an unexpected trip, you can simply read down your list of things to pack and grab your reminder card to lessen your anxiety—and the risk of leaving without something important.

You might also create a list of things to accomplish at work before leaving so you're not constantly worrying about the office when you're away. While planning, attend to your personal life as well, and think of ways to ease your return. You might plan to have your home cleaned when you're away, or purchase tickets to a cultural event for the week you get back.

Make your travel plans as early as possible. Take advantage of your company's corporate travel department, or find yourself a first-class travel agent to help you schedule your trip. If there's some flexibility on when you leave, time your trip to avoid big conventions, crowds, and peak travel times. Provide your agent with a list of your personal preferences for airlines, travel times, seating, and accommodations. Ask your agent to prepare contingency travel plans, including alternative train or plane schedules, along with directions and the best mode of transportation to where you'll be staying. Obtain from your travel agent a 24-hour toll-free number in case of last-minute changes. Consider taking along the *Official Airline Guide* pocket or electronic editions published by Official Airline Guides, 2000 Clearwater Drive, Oakbrook, Ill. 60521, (800) 323-4000, for information on available alternative flights. It also helps to put your itinerary and meeting schedule in writing and distribute it to key people at work, family, and friends. That way, you can be reached during an emergency.

Plan ahead to meet the particular stressors of concern to you which you have identified as within your control. For example, if you've missed morning appointments in the past because the hotel alarm clock didn't work, pack your own. Kathy Levinson, senior vice president at Charles Schwab in San Francisco, learned early on that downtime at airports and on the plane caused her stress. To cope with waiting time, she now travels with a portable computer and reading material that she purposefully allows to pile up at work before a trip. Flying home, she prepares a report of her trip on her laptop computer. Are there key phone calls you can make from the airport or train station? What about reviewing nonessential mail that's been stacking up? If working during downtime isn't for you, pack a good novel, your diary, or music tapes.

Your foray into a new place will be less stressful the more you know about it, especially if you're a first-time traveler to a new country. "Our view is that Americanism *is* the world culture," said travel researcher Stanley Plog in an interview with *USA Today*. But if we break through our provincial shells and gain an understanding of the local customs, foods, and habits before leaving, cultural differences will seem more intriguing than annoying. Take the time to peruse a guidebook, obtain personal recommendations, or clip travel articles. Many companies and on-line computer services now sell travel information. For example, Fodor's Worldview Update offers current information by fax on about 180 cities worldwide. If you're headed to Paris next week and want to know a good jogging route or need a schedule of the week's cultural events, *presto*, Fodor faxes the information in 48 hours for about $7.

Don't miss opportunities for culture and adventure even if you're just traveling domestically. "Get familiar with the city you're traveling to so you can look forward to it," advises Denise Bruns of San Diego, who travels more than 150,000 miles a year as a research manager for Molecular Biosystems. "Even Tiffin, Ohio, offers things to see and do. If you make your inquiries and have an evening to yourself, you can make it a better time instead of going to your hotel room and being miserable because you're alone."

Contact the state tourism office or local chamber of commerce to discover activities at your destination in case you have some free time. Or find ways to mix business with pleasure. Be creative. You might hold a business meeting at a local museum or cultural landmark. We suggest keeping files on different cities highlighting the options offered by each. Where are the best restaurants? Historic neighborhoods? Places for an evening stroll?

The more you know about the place, the more possibility for having fun when a block of time unexpectedly comes available while in transit or between business commitments. Avid golfer Ed Dandridge, a strategic consultant for a New York consulting firm, filed away the location of a driving range near Chicago's O'Hare Airport. When faced with a three-hour layover, he took a cab to the driving range, hit balls for an hour, got back into the cab, and made his flight.

# Pace Yourself

Trying to do too much in too little time causes major travel stress. So many travelers set unrealistic goals of what they plan to achieve while away. Certainly, there's more pressure now than ever before to justify the expense of a business trip by having every minute scheduled, but at some point enough is enough. You're not doing your employer or yourself any good by making critical decisions or closing key deals while frazzled or pressured. To keep clear-headed and effective, pacing yourself is key.

Pacing requires a sense of priorities. What do you really need to accomplish on this trip? Eliminate from your itinerary anything nonessential. If you begin to feel that your trip is running you, slow down by cutting out a less important task. For example, if you're stressed midway through a trip, cancel a relatively unimportant evening function and take some time for yourself. You'll perform much better the next day.

Schedule travel plans and set appointments so you're not over-booked. Always build in a margin for error by allowing plenty of time at the airport or train station and between meetings. There's nothing worse than trying to catch the last flight out and running into weather delays. "Because many businesspeople don't want any downtime, they end up scheduling things so close that they have a lot more downtime than they ever anticipated," says Dr. Goldstein. "A one-hour layover turns into eight hours of waiting because of a missed connection."

Absolutely never overschedule your first day, especially if you've crossed several time zones. You need some time to adjust to the new place and to recuperate from travel. We can't emphasize this point enough. Ideally, arrive a day or two early. But even catching an early morning flight and allowing an hour or two to yourself after arriving will help. Similarly, at the back end, give yourself at least a day at home to adjust before returning to work.

Take a look at your performance on more extended stays. The Hyatt study showed that most business travelers maintain their effectiveness while traveling for four or five days. After five days, two-thirds of those surveyed felt that their business effectiveness diminished. If you need to perform at your peak, try planning two or three short excursions rather than one marathon trip, and take enough time in between to recuperate.

# Keep a Routine

As exciting as change is, our bodies crave the old ways. There are only so many behavioral adaptations each of us can make on any given trip without feeling the negative effects of stress. It's as if we each carry with us our own personalized travel-stress budget, our maximum allotment of endurable annoyances. When our budget is overtaxed, we're going to feel depleted. You can, however, temper the amount of adjustment your body and psyche must accomplish by maintaining some of your at-home patterns of sleeping, eating, and exercising when traveling. If you always have a certain kind of food at a certain time at home, pack a little of it with you and indulge at your usual hour. If your head hits the pillow in your hotel room the same time it does at home, that's one less change your body must cope with. You'll have more of your stress budget to spend elsewhere, like adjusting to—and enjoying—the local culture.

How religiously you choose to adhere to your at-home habits to prevent overload may depend on the size of your personal stress budget. Given your body type and temperament, how much change can you tolerate without succumbing to fatigue and poor performance? If you can trot across the globe, eat exotic cuisine, miss a night's sleep, and still ace tomorrow's business meeting, maybe you can toss your routines to the wind. But if you're like most of us, being on automatic pilot at least for part of the trip sure helps.

For Dr. Margaret Chesney, a clinical psychologist and professor in the School of Medicine at the University of San Francisco, keeping her at-home routines helps to cue her body and mind to adjust to a new place and time. "The minute I arrive I will begin to exercise as I would if I were home. If I arrive and it's evening, the time I normally exercise at home, I get right into my routine. That really helps my body realize it's evening time," she says.

You might even take reminders and comforts from home to transform your new environment into a personal comfort zone. Toting your flannel sheets, favorite pajamas, pictures of family or friends, or music tapes that evoke happy memories help to create a sense of security and familiarity. One traveler takes a wonderful letter her father wrote to her years ago and reads it when she's feeling stressed. Dr. Joyce Brothers, who admits to trouble sleeping her first night in a new environment, brings her own soft feather pillow.

While honoring some of your at-home routines, consider starting a new set of special travel rituals—little things you do every time before leaving home or while you're away to ease into travel or to help you relax when you're away. If repeated over several trips, travel rituals can provide security in their own right. Some travelers start a new book at the beginning of each trip or write in their diary each day they're gone. Or you might take a hot shower as soon as you arrive, or stretch every morning and evening in your hotel room without fail. If you've found a good restaurant in a city and happen to be back in town, go back to the same place. When everything else conspires to rob you of your sense of control, your travel rituals can provide safe harbors of tranquility that preserve your sanity on the road.

## Find Time for Yourself

The frazzled traveler who sets aside 10 to 20 minutes every day of the trip to take a break and, if possible, just do nothing will gain an edge on stress. There's a simple rule of nature that most of us are too busy to discover: our bodies naturally unwind when left alone. Under stress, blood pressure rises, the heart beats faster, metabolism races, and breathing quickens. But everyone also "possesses a natural and innate protective mechanism against over-stress, which allows us to turn off harmful bodily effects, to counter the effects of the fight-or-flight response," says Dr. Benson. We each can invoke what he calls the "relaxation response," a physiologic condition diametrically opposed to the bodily hyper-drive associated with stress. The relaxation response is characterized by decreased heart rate and metabolism, lessened oxygen consumption, and lowered blood pressure.

Many techniques—from autogenic training, progressive muscle relaxation, and visualization to transcendental meditation, Zen, yoga, deep breathing, and hypnosis—induce the mental and physical calm of the relaxation response. "People who regularly elicit the relaxation response can counteract the harmful effects of travel stress," says Benson. All of these techniques have four principal elements in common:

1. A quiet environment;

2. Repetition of a word, phrase, prayer, sound, image, or something else to focus on;

3. A passive attitude; and

4. A comfortable position.

Finding your own way to practice daily each of these four elements will help you prepare for and deal with the many unalterable stresses of travel. Says Rajiv Tandon of St. Paul, Minnesota, who logs 250,000 miles a year traveling: "I meditate at home, but on the road I make it a point to meditate every day. It's a life saver."

For others the mere thought of sitting quietly alone for 10 to 20 minutes is excruciating. Just as each of us responds differently to stress, no single stress-reduction technique works for everyone. For those whose blood pressure rises at the mention of "doing nothing," exercise provides a great means to reduce stress build-ups. It not only provides physical and emotional release from stress but induces physiologic calm by triggering the release of endorphins. Adding a cognitive element to muscular activity provides added benefits, advises Dr. Benson. "There are many ways of eliciting the relaxation response, and it need not be sitting quietly. You could elicit it while exercising. The repetitive nature of your jogging—left, right, left, right—can induce calm." Even a light stroll can immediately untangle your nerves if you use simple mental techniques. A recent study by Ruth Stricker, owner and director of The Marsh: A Center for Balance in Minnetonka, Minnesota, and Dr. Rippe, showed that slow walkers who practiced the relaxation response by counting their steps and visualizing the numbers as they walked gained the same positive effects as brisk walkers. Both groups experienced decreases in anxiety and fewer negative and more positive feelings about themselves—effects that kicked in after just one exercise session. The slow walkers who did not invoke the relaxation response gained no benefits until the 14th week of the study and then the benefits weren't as extensive.

Examples of other travel stress relievers that you can accomplish in 20 minutes or less include taking a nap; enjoying a Jacuzzi, hot bath, or shower; listening to a relaxation tape or soothing music; stretching in your hotel; or writing in a journal. Denise Bruns always asks for a suite upgrade to take advantage of "those tremendous jetted Jacuzzi tubs. It's very relaxing and therapeutic." Experiment to see what works for you.

# TRAVEL FITNESS TIPS:
# GIVE YOURSELF A BREAK

This may strike some as frivolous or self-indulgent. After all, we're in the decade of the lean and mean '90s where travel budgets have been slashed to the bone. Naysayers aside, we believe that scheduling at least one fun thing to do per trip *unrelated to work* will improve your performance and increase your enthusiasm for travel. You can mix business with a little pleasure—without raising the cost to your employer. On every trip there are moments, if not hours, of aimless free time. The challenge for the traveler is to transform those moments into relaxing personal time. "Business travel is an intense, high-stress time," notes Peter Dubow, an independent marketing consultant, in an interview with *Hemispheres* magazine. "You'd be foolish if you didn't take advantage of those moments that slip through the cracks to relax and recharge your batteries. It will improve your performance in the end."

Has a block of unexpected time become available? Then take your blinders off and look around. Play tourist for an hour or two. If you've kept track of enticing excursions, you shouldn't have a problem figuring out what to do. On a trip to San Antonio, Texas, Dr. Chesney squeezed in a walk to the Alamo during a two-hour break between meetings and a business dinner. "It's easy to say you don't have the energy, but if there's something special to do in town, do it. It will really add to your trip," she says.

Are you an amateur photographer? An avid bird watcher? Taking your camera or binoculars along could make your trip infinitely more endurable. Is there any way to squeeze in a massage, facial, or manicure? What about excusing yourself from that demanding boss or client for an entire evening? (A well-timed reference to the work you brought along serves as a handy excuse). You could entertain yourself with your laptop or soak in a hot bath with a glass of wine. Many spas now offer two-day packages. Consider extending your stay over the weekend for a real pampering adventure. Not only might you save company money with an advance-purchase discount airfare requiring a Saturday night stayover, you'll return home feeling great and ready to work. Many companies reward employees taking the lower fares by picking up some of the tab on extra hotel and meal costs (of course, the spa charges come out of your pocketbook). If you're in another country, is there something tempting nearby? Use accumulated frequent-flier mileage to fly in a friend or spouse for an instant vacation. There's simply no reason to feel guilty about taking a break.

## Social Support on the Road

Feeling like just another face in the crowd distorts and exaggerates the stress of travel. If you're traveling alone, becoming involved with others, preferably people you like, is a great antidote to stress. "Studies show that social contact may lower pulse rate and blood pressure, enhance the immune system and boost the production of endorphins, neurochemicals that make us feel good," says Dr. Raymond Flannery Jr., assistant clinical professor of psychology at Harvard University Medical School, in an interview with *American Health* magazine.

Spending more time with an irascible co-worker won't reduce your stress, but getting together with old friends or college alumni in the area could be a fun adventure. Tapping into national organizations related to your field is another way to meet people where you're staying. This is an especially good way for women to overcome the social restraints of being out on the road alone. The Hyatt study showed that travel takes a greater toll on women under 35 and women with children. The difficulty in coping with separation from home life and concerns for personal security are of key concern to women. Many women we interviewed for this book became prisoners of their hotel rooms while traveling, surviving on room service and only venturing out to conduct business. As one female traveler put it: "I have no problem being a woman so long as I don't have to go anywhere." To overcome her inhibitions as a woman traveling alone, Dr. Clare Elizabeth Carey, a management consultant from Columbia, Maryland, contacts the president of the local chapter of the National Society of Performance and Instruction, to ascertain whether any meetings or events are on the agenda for when she's in town. She's usually able to fit at least one professional dinner into her trip. "I still want a social life when I'm on the road. I've been able to expand my professional contacts and make new friends across the country," she says.

Joining special airline and hotel clubs is another good way to meet people in a relatively safe environment. Even something as simple as dining at a Benihana-style restaurant, where you're guaranteed dining companions, helps to combat loneliness.

# On the Home Front: The Stress of Separation

Leaving a spouse, child, significant relationship, or friends has emotional consequences for the traveler and those left behind. Experts say absence may not make the heart grow fonder; in fact, repeated separations over a long period can erode the bond in any relationship. Although some may share George Bernard Shaw's view that the "great advantage of a hotel is that it is a refuge from home life," experiencing some degree of separation stress is the norm. When you're accustomed to the daily companionship and comfort of an intimate relationship, having it abruptly taken away is disconcerting. Single parents and dual-career couples with young children are particularly challenged by frequent travel because of child-care responsibilities.

The intensity of the response to separation depends on personal history, the characteristics of the relationship, and situational factors. Typically, the longer the separation and the closer the attachment between the couple, the more difficult coping becomes. Well-spaced shorter trips can actually provide welcome time alone, but long trips or too many trips in too short of a period are stressful.

Research on wartime and job-related marital separations shows that the departing spouse and the one at home have very different emotional responses. Studies suggest that the differing response patterns are not gender-specific, but rather have more to do with whether you're the one leaving or staying at home. The traveling partner primarily feels guilt, although he or she may also feel lonely and anxious. For the person left behind, the partner's departure triggers predictable grief-like stages of protest, despair, and detachment. He or she may progress through a gamut of emotions from loneliness, tension, and mood changes to sleep disturbances and resentment. Of course there are significant individual differences, but these tendencies are important to note.

At an emotional level "any separation from an attachment figure brings with it the threat of losing the person and of being unprotected for the moment and perhaps abandoned in the long run," writes separation researcher Julia K. Vormbrock in a recent article in the *Psychological Bulletin.* "Despite the short absences of the spouse, feelings of loneliness and sometimes even depression have been identified in wives of traveling executives." While the traveler explores, the at-home loved one unconsciously responds as if the wanderer may never return. Recovery for the person at home ultimately requires an element of emotional distancing or detachment where the spouse reinvents his or her daily routine, often relying on close relatives and friends to fill the gap.

In the pages that follow, we discuss what happens in intimate relationships before and during separation and the best ways to handle it. Just knowing that certain responses are predictable frees us to cope with the sometimes intense emotions evoked by separation.

## Before You Go

News of an upcoming business trip is often greeted with a bit of anger or expressed dissatisfaction from those staying behind: "Do you have to leave, again? You just came back from a trip!" During this "protest" stage, those at home may also feel numb, denying the pending departure. They may busy themselves with extra work and activities, acting as if nothing is wrong. The traveler also experiences letting-go anxiety in many ways, says Richard J. Leider, partner in The Inventure Group, a Minneapolis-based training and consulting firm, and author of *Lifeskills: Taking Charge of Your Personal and Professional Growth* (1993). As the departure date nears, the traveler becomes increasingly preoccupied with preparing for the trip. The traveler is emotionally unavailable, which further strains the relationship. What's more, tension "increases dramatically if a traveler leaves town on a weekend. Many buried feelings can surface on the way to the airport on a Saturday or Sunday. Families feel terribly inconvenienced by work needs that impinge on their precious weekend time," says Leider.

## Separation

Although myths of the glamour of business travel abound, during the separation stage, both the traveler and the family at home feel that they suffer the most. Both parties may be concerned about the sexual fidelity and new-found freedom of the other partner. The traveler may feel guilty and concerned about the family's safety while facing the many stresses of conducting business on the road. Other travelers feel lonely and dislocated. One male executive attributed his trouble sleeping on the road to his wife not being with him. Missing significant family events such as birthdays and anniversaries is also difficult.

For the home-based person, protest gives way to loneliness, even depression, anxiety, and anger. "My traveling is very hard on my husband. He doesn't like my being gone," says Denise Bruns. "I have to deal with his grief of being home alone." At an emotional level, the necessity of the trip doesn't seem to matter; the only reality is that the cherished loved one is unavailable. Anxiety about security concerns is also common among those left behind, especially women. Many report checking the locks on windows and doors several times at night before going to bed. Having a security system installed helps to ease such anxiety.

Meanwhile, daily home life must go on. Decision making, finances, and child care are shouldered entirely by the person at home. This is an opportunity for the at-home partner to gain skills in areas traditionally the domain of the other spouse. But having to do it all may cause resentment. Saddled with responsibilities, the spouse at home may view the traveler as footloose and fancy-free. How much difficulty the person at home experiences depends on how equally respective roles have been worked out. Stress and disorganization can occur if the traveler refuses to relinquish some control by creating unworkable restrictions like "don't make any major decisions when I'm gone"— and then departs for three weeks. Stressful events during separation, like pregnancy or having a sick or injured child at home, further hinder adjustment. Couples also find that mending disagreements at a distance is a bit like tiptoeing through a mine field. One woman in a commuter relationship who had just argued with her boyfriend over the phone lamented, "We'll just have to wait until we see each other again to make it right."

To cope, the person at home typically reverts to his or her pre-relationship way of doing things, subtly detaching from the traveler. "With respect to couples in corporate business, a tendency to close out the absent spouse is evident in both a practical and an emotional sense," writes Vormbrock. Over repeated absences, the person at home may create a lifestyle that's not dependent on the other being around. What particularly helps the person at home is time with close relatives, although social contact with friends and acquaintances provides a distraction and an opportunity to talk about pent-up feelings. Those who cope the best tend to daily life but remain emotionally open to the traveling partner.

# Four Ways to Travel
## *and* Take Care of Your Relationships

You may be thinking, I *have to travel for my job*. How can I cope with the emotional fallout from separation? Fortunately, accommodating travel demands and family life isn't an either/or proposition. You and your relationships can thrive despite a fairly hectic travel schedule. How? By learning responses that help build relationships. Here are four useful guides to help you nurture your important relationships when your lifestyle demands a good dose of travel.

## *1. Communicate*

If being on the road is about as much fun as visiting the dentist, but your partner conjures images of you luxuriating over six-course meals in exotic cities, the stage is set for unnecessary conflict. Suppressed communication—what is felt, but unsaid—is the offender behind most travel-related tension, says Leider. "Every family is different, but for each, sitting down and facing the issues—What are our roles? When are we going to get time together as a couple? How do each of us really experience our time apart? What is needed to cope?—is key," he says. "Families need to talk about what's needed and expected rather than assuming it's going to get handled, because most times it won't."

Being gone too often, without day-to-day interaction, taxes the relationship between partners with the best communication skills. This makes it all the more important to develop a shared understanding of travel, so each of you carry a common framework for coping. At a minimum, expressing losses, fears, and disappointments lets some steam out of the kettle before it boils over.

Communicating from afar can be a challenging, yet creative, undertaking. Daily contact over the telephone is absolutely necessary for keeping your relationship stable. (Some companies even pick up the extra phone costs for employees who call home). Leaving your itinerary, a list of telephone numbers where you can be reached, and as many details of the trip as possible helps your family stay connected. But just reaching out and touching someone isn't always as simple as it would seem. Some novice travelers, for example, promise to call at a specific time; then something unpredictable happens, and they can't get to a phone. The partner at home imagines the worst.

Then there's the complication of getting your point across without face-to-face contact. One wife described a recent telephone conversation with her out-of-town husband during which she "hung on every word" and construed subtle changes in tone as a problem in the relationship. After the phone call, she felt uneasy until she spoke with him again the next night. Given the opportunity for crossed signals, solving major life issues or conflicts over the telephone isn't the best idea. But you don't want to communicate only on a practical, superficial level either. This might worsen the feelings of separation. Finding creative ways to comfort each other really helps. For Kathleen Gedeon, having her husband put their purring cats on the phone gives her solace from home. "It settles me down every time," she says.

You can communicate without ever picking up the phone. When Dr. Margaret Chesney traveled for her annual business trip to Russia for two weeks, during which telephone contact with her husband was nearly impossible, she solved the communication crisis by hiding notes for him around the house that he was certain to find. The next year he reciprocated by arranging photographs from their album, starting from when they first met to the present, for her to take on her trip. "He told me to open the envelope in a certain way and to look at one picture each day. When it was time to come home, I was looking at pictures of times we recently shared," she says.

Consider making your presence felt at home by sending flowers or, like Dr. Eric Goldstein, leaving tapes behind. He has twin daughters at home in Miami, who love bedtime stories. "I'll make a tape for them before I leave of Little Red Riding Hood or The Three Bears, and my wife will play it for them at night. Even though Dad's not there, at least they can hear Daddy telling them stories."

## 2. Build Flexible Roles and an Equal Power-Sharing Structure

The less rigid the roles are in your relationship, the more capable each of you will be to pinch-hit for the other when one of you leaves town. There's nothing worse for the person at home than having his or her hands tied when it comes to making decisions and handling daily life. The family structure can unravel into chaos when the person at home keeps relying on the absent partner. The separation period, however, need not be so stressful, says Dr. Frederic J. Medway, professor of psychology at the University of South Carolina and an expert on intermittent separation. "But it's going to depend on how you've negotiated roles and responsibilities. If the traveler doesn't give a lot of responsibility to the person at home, you're going to have potential problems during separation. We advocate that marriages be as equal as possible and that there be shared responsibility so that both partners can do any number of things," he says.

## 3. Draw Your Travel Boundaries

How often and for how long can a person be gone and still be part of a fully functioning family? This, says Leider, is the central question each family must answer for itself. "But rarely do they actually sit down and do that," he says. "People just assume that there's no choice. The fact is people can ask themselves: What are our major priorities? What are the boundaries across which we will not go? If you're not clear on your priorities, then you'll always break them."

Since Dr. Goldstein's twin daughters arrived, he refuses to stay away for more than a night or two. "Otherwise I feel that I'm going to miss some of their development," he says. Tim McCarthy of Mentor, Ohio, who travels 150,000 miles a year and is often gone four or five days a week, also has put the brakes on some of his traveling. In an interview with *USA Today*, he said he feels "impending doom" at the thought of leaving his wife and three children behind. His family's solution: no more weekend travel, more day trips so he's back at home at night, and more fun weekend trips together. Or, like Claire Diorio-Schultz, you may decide travel isn't worth it anymore. A mother of three, she traveled around the country as a sales representative before calling it quits. "I just can't do it anymore," she said in an interview with the *Wall Street Journal.* Luckily her company decided to keep her on board, promoting her to a management job.

If you feel that your home has become just a place to store your clothes, Leider suggests these ways to scale back your travel itinerary:

- Carefully analyze the purpose and length of each trip. IBM now encourages its managers to teleconference or to consider shorter trips whenever possible. Some consulting firms, notorious for placing extreme travel demands on their employees, have at least cut their consultants' travel schedules to keep weekends sacred. Is there any other way to get the job done without going? Will a written report supplemented with a telephone call substitute for being there in person? Can the trip be shortened without sacrificing work quality and personal productivity? Decline unnecessary trips and limit travel whenever possible.
- Preserve reasonable time periods between trips.

- If at all possible, avoid travel on weekends, holidays, birthdays, anniversaries, and other special occasions.

One of the best ways to approach your boss with requests to limit travel is to couch them in terms of cost-containment and efficiency: If you travel less and still get the job done, you'll save the company money. Even the most difficult manager appreciates an employee's dedication to the company's bottom line. Let's say, for example, that your boss suggests you attend a four-day training seminar in another city. With a little research, you discover that a videotaped version of the course is available. Suggesting the videotapes spares you and your family a four-day separation and demonstrates your loyalty to the company's goals.

## 4. Take Them With You

Taking your spouse, significant other, children, or friends along when the city seems promising is a great antidote to the separation blues. Why not cash in some of those frequent-flier miles to fly your loved one in, especially if otherwise you'll miss a birthday, anniversary, or other special affair? "Taking every opportunity to have family members with you attenuates some of the stress of travel and helps you do things that you might not otherwise do," says Dr. Harry Levinson, a psychologist and chairman of the Levinson Institute in Waltham, Massachusetts. Dr. Levinson, whose business travels have taken him to Australia, New Zealand, Thailand, Bali, and South Africa in one year, brings his wife along on any trip longer than overnight. Of course, a week in an industrial outpost with nothing to do may leave a spouse questioning his or her decision to tag along. So ask yourself: Does this city interest us? Will there be enough for my partner to do when I'm tending to business?

A growing number of working parents travel on business with their children in tow as a way to fit in precious family time. In 1991, 9 percent of all business travelers brought their children along, up from 3 percent in 1987, according to the U.S. Travel Data Center. Some travelers combine a work week with a weekend stayover that's purely a vacation for the family. You may discover the extra travel costs of bringing your young children won't put much of a dent in your pocketbook. Many hotels now offer child-proofed rooms; provide free diaper pails, strollers, and cribs; and allow up to two kids to stay in their parents' room at no extra charge. Others operate baby-sitting programs and on-site camps for kids. There are even frequent-flier programs for children. Ask your travel agent for information on available mileage programs and the names of child-friendly hotels where you're headed. Or contact Travel With Your Children, 80 Eighth Avenue, New York, NY 10011, (212) 206-0688, an organization that helps travelers find hotels that cater to kids.

# What to Do When Travel Stress Strikes

You're 2,000 miles away from home and the support of family and friends. The unexpected happens. Your body sounds the alarm. How can you stop, or at least allay, the negative spiral of stress? Here are five simple tips to remember.

## 1. Observe Yourself

The first step in handling stress is to recognize that you're feeling it in the first place. Often while traveling we are so focused on getting the next thing done that we don't appreciate how our bodies are responding in the moment. Is your face flushed? Has your breathing quickened? Do you feel your heart pounding? You're probably primed to fight or flee. Once aware of stress signals, you can take measures to calm yourself and change your experience of it.

## 2. Keep Breathing

Taking several deep breaths is an immediate stress-buster. Your brain and muscles need adequate oxygen intake to perform well. The shallow breathing associated with the fight-or-flight response causes oxygen-deprived muscles to tense and the brain to cloud over. "Your stress response hinges on your breath," writes Dr. Robert K. Cooper in *Health and Fitness Excellence*. "By changing the way you breathe, you can change the way you think and feel. When you notice stress signals—tense muscles, cold hands, irregular breathing, rapid pulse, nervous sweating—use smooth, deep breathing to regain control."

What people often don't realize is that deep breathing and relaxation techniques create positive physiological change, says Dr. Goldstein. "You're reducing your heart rate, blood pressure, and muscle tension. It's not just a psychological benefit."

You might also invoke your preferred stress management technique to enhance your breathing, advises Dr. Goldstein. If you visualize at home, imagine yourself relaxing on a beach and take in a few deep breaths. You can go anywhere you want, hassle-free, for a three- to five-minute mental vacation.

## 3. Watch What You Tell Yourself

While traveling, we tend to exaggerate and feel threatened by otherwise insignificant events. Watch for negative thought patterns that create needless stress. Some stress-inducing responses to avoid include overreacting ("The plane is late; my trip is ruined"), all-or-nothing thinking ("I didn't perform at my best today; I'll never handle business travel"), or blaming ("I can't enjoy business travel because the airlines always mess up"). Avoiding such negative interpretations of events will help you keep your perspective.

## 4. Focus on Finding a Solution

People who deal the best with stress take control of the events causing stress whenever possible, says Dr. Flannery, who conducted a 12-year study on people's ability to resist stress. When travel stress strikes, travelers stay in the present and look for ways to either solve the problem or accept the situation with grace. OK, the hotel room that you booked a month ago has been given away. Why waste your energy in a screaming match with the clerk or conjuring images of sleeping on a park bench in a strange city? Accept the mistake and move on to problem solving as soon as possible. Given this situation, what are your options? Ask to speak directly to the manager. Is there another room available? Where's the next best hotel? Can the manager call ahead and reserve a room for you? With your energy directed toward problem solving, you'll usually find a solution you can live with.

## 5. Be Assertive!

Let's say your taxi driver gets lost and decides to charge you double fare. How you respond dramatically influences the level of stress you'll feel. Do you pay without comment, secretly seething inside? Or do you calmly express your dissatisfaction and negotiate a reasonable rate? The former response probably will leave you feeling taken advantage of and angry, adding to the stress of an already negative experience. The latter response puts you in the driver's seat and lessens the amount of stress you'll experience. Learning to say no and to stand up for yourself are two crucial steps toward keeping your stress level in check.

# The Travel Stress Checklist

Keep these tips in mind the next time travel stresses you out:

❑ Make a list of travel stressors and brainstorm ways to overcome those you can control.

❑ Focus on the positive opportunities travel provides you.

❑ Practice the art of superb preparation.

❑ Have your travel agent prepare contingency travel plans.

❑ Learn as much as you can about your destination before leaving.

❑ Prioritize what you need to accomplish on the trip.

❑ Always build in a margin for error between travel connections and meetings.

❑ Never overschedule your first day.

❑ Adhere to some of your at-home eating, sleeping, and exercising routines.

❑ Pack reminders and comforts from home.

❑ For 15 to 20 minutes a day, do nothing.

❑ Schedule one fun activity per trip.

❑ Seek out social support on the road.

❑ Discuss with family members the difficulties of travel and brainstorm ways to cope.

❑ Create travel boundaries.

❑ Occasionally take your family with you.

❑ If possible, call home every day.

❑ When something goes wrong, focus on finding a solution.

❑ Keep breathing.

❑ Be assertive.

# Coming Home Strong

> "Most people know the feeling. You've been away someplace, had a great time. You get home and, before you can even unpack your souvenirs, dreary old problems surface, dreary new problems crowd in, and soon some…person—all right, some wacko—asks who's been minding the store."
>
> Andy Logan
> *New Yorker,* April 9, 1984

**Y**ou've flitted across time zones, braved endless throngs and snarls of traffic, all to reach your final destination—home. After days of unrelenting change, you find comfort in the thought of settling into your domestic and work routines. Yet on returning home, making the transition into your daily life isn't as easy as you imagined it would be. You feel like a stranger in your own home. Work has piled up on the job, but you resist delving into it. And you struggle to reestablish your workout and fitness routines.

Many returning travelers underestimate the challenge of readjusting to family and work life. Coming home can trigger an emotional and physical letdown in some travelers. Each of us responds differently, but many returning travelers report feeling unmotivated, disoriented, and/or distant. Travel, as we have seen, is a heightened, even peak, experience for some. Returning to the routines of home and office can feel downright pedestrian, and it requires an adjustment. For others, a mild grief reaction can be part of the letdown after a trip. "If it's been a good trip, there's always going to be a sense of loss," notes Dr. Aaron Kulick, an instructor of psychiatry at Harvard Medical School, in an interview with *Travel & Leisure* magazine. "You've seen new places, and perhaps you've met new friends, and you have to say goodbye. It's a very mild grief reaction, and you have to mourn in some way. Traveling gives you a chance to try out new roles, to create yourself differently, to be whoever you want to be. No matter how satisfying your life is, there's still an element of fantasy in traveling that's hard to emulate."

The reentry experience also can be associated with some level of fatigue from "residual tiredness" and "losing my edge" to "feeling dead." As one traveler put it: "It's not my age, it's the mileage. This body has been around—and feels the effects." There's no question that traveling is hard work. While conscientious self-management helps minimize the impact of travel on our well-being, the rigors of the road and the letdown of ending a trip nevertheless can cause fatigue. Sometimes the adrenaline infusion that propels a traveler through a grueling trip vanishes after returning home. It's as if the plug has been pulled on your energy reserves. "I always find it much harder to adjust when I get back home," says Seattle-based traveler Steve Campbell. "The adrenaline got me pumped up and kept me going during the business trip, but when I get home, I'm drained."

Is an initial period of malaise inevitable after a trip? Absolutely not. In this chapter, we'll share practical strategies for coming home strong emotionally and physically to family and work and the best ways to resume your fitness routines.

# Building Bridges

To let go of a trip and reconnect with the environment at home, travelers often go through a type of "reentry routine." They may perform certain habitual activities that serve as transition rituals, emotional bridges between two widely different experiences. Many travelers, like Jacqui Wolfe, of Reston, Virginia, who takes 30 to 35 trips a year as a health-care consultant, immediately unpack. No matter what the time of day, they want their bags out of sight. "As soon as possible I unpack and get rid of my suitcase. I just don't want any reminders," she says. Others putter around the house, sorting through the mail, watering the plants, tackling paperwork, or housecleaning. John C. Kauphusman takes another tack: he instantly reactivates his social life to get back the routine. "Usually the trips from Asia get me home in the morning. The first thing I do is get on the phone and call friends to say I'm back. It helps me feel connected again." Woo Daves may have the best reentry routine of all. Even after a week or more of professional fishing, he comes home for a little more. "The first thing I do is get in my boat and go out catfishing to relax, just to get away from everything for awhile. I want to leave the planes, the cars, the endless roadway behind," he says.

What do you do to help connect again with home? Whether quirky or mundane, the reentry rituals you observe actually help you psychologically ease back into your routine.

## Returning to Your Family

The honeymoon reunion is more the product of Hollywood fantasy than day-to-day reality. "If there's one point to be made about business travel conflict, it's that it's most likely to occur when people get back together," says Dr. Frederic J. Medway, professor of psychology at the University of South Carolina. But why? Part of the reason is that during the separation, the traveler and the person at home live on their own terms and experience different realities. There's a gulf between the respective experiences of the traveler and the stay-at-home partner that has to be bridged. Each has missed out on a part of the other's life. Until they spend time together catching up, many couples initially feel distant or unnatural around each other. Psychologists label this the "stranger effect." Says Bill Wood, a veteran traveler from Harrison, Maine: "We each get into our own routines when I'm on the road. My wife has her way of doing things, and I have mine. When I come home we have to get in sync again."

Negotiating the differences takes time, maybe even an argument or two. "The first time my husband left for about a month, it was really hard when he came home. It was like: 'Why do you have to do that with the remote control?' I was just really used to having everything on my terms," says Susan McFadden, of San Francisco, whose husband Maury travels frequently as a U.S. Coast Guard officer. If children are involved, tiffs over discipline are common. One spouse reported not feeling comfortable around her husband until after their first fight.

Creating even more opportunity for friction, the returning traveler and the person at home typically have very different emotional reactions and needs at reunion. "Returning spouses tend to be eager to resume intimacy, even if it means that they have to appease their resentful partner," writes Julia K. Vormbrock in the *Psychological Bulletin.* The family, however, may not abruptly alter their schedules to accommodate the returning road warrior. "In contrast, home-based spouses seem to feel torn between feelings of irritation and a desire for closeness with their spouse." Ironically, home-based spouses who cope the best during separation may have a tougher time at reunion, notes Vormbrock. To survive the separation, they may have distanced themselves too far, making reunion difficult. Having assumed most of the household responsibilities during the absence, the stay-at-home spouse feels preempted when the traveler returns and again exerts his or her influence. At the extreme, the person at home views the traveling spouse as intruding on his or her routine. (When this degree of detachment develops, you might consider retiring your suitcase to the closet for good.) Often feeling worn down and somewhat bitter, the person at home may even harbor an unconscious desire to punish the traveler for leaving. When the traveler focuses exclusively on the children, work, or friends at reunion, tension mounts.

Despite the increased risk for conflict, reunion can be a happy ending when couples focus on each other after a trip. Research shows that much of the non-traveler's resentment evaporates when the returning spouse compensates him or her by paying special attention or doing extra work around the house. To maintain harmony at home, make time alone with your partner a priority after a trip. Before you depart, schedule a block of relationship time after your return that's untouchable so that each of you has something to look forward to. Try to plan something that will work for both of you. After a trip, you may desire a quiet dinner at home, while your spouse, feeling housebound, may want a night on the town. Maybe a dinner date at a favorite restaurant the second night back is a workable option. Ideally, during this time alone you and your partner can acknowledge each other's efforts and catch up on what your days were like while apart. Remember, the partner at home likely feels a little more conflict about the reunion. Focusing on each other, pitching in around the house, or doing other "extras" will help the stay-at-home partner overcome feelings of distance and resentment. "What came up in our interviews with spouses who stayed at home is that the worst thing the traveler can do is to walk through the door and say, 'Where's the mail?'" says Dr. Medway. "The person at home wants the traveler to spend time with him or her. The one thing they want to be told when the traveler comes back home is that they were missed and that they are loved. They want to feel that they are appreciated for the sacrifices that they made during the travel. If you can do that, I think everything else will follow nicely."

Another important way to reduce tension at reunion is to focus on easing back into family life. Craving intimacy, many travelers rush headlong into their relationships and family life, blind to the routines that have grown up in their absence. Expecting your partner or child to act as if you never left is unrealistic—and sets you up for disappointment. Remember that the folks at home may have become somewhat self-contained to cope with your absence. "Life went on, and family members don't suddenly alter their schedules because Mom or Dad is coming home," says Richard J. Leider, an expert on travel separation. Go slow, and be patient with yourself and others. Says Bill Wood: "I've learned not to come barging through the door and say, 'Honey, let's do this or that.' I give it time." Make it a rule to listen to your family first before regaling them with details of your trip. "When you come home, listen! listen! listen! before you share your hero's journey," writes Leider. Try observing changes without immediately taking up the reins, especially where disciplining the children is concerned. Avoid undoing reasonable rules set by your spouse in your absence. For example, granting your teenager's request for a new pair of skis (possibly to ease your guilt?) when your spouse already said no may not be in anyone's best interest.

## Returning to Your Work

If you do feel tired or disoriented after a trip and just can't get with it at work, what's the best way to cope? For starters, accept the cues your body sends you. Some people underestimate the battering their body and psyche take on a typical trip. Maybe the constraints of the trip made it impossible for you to observe even a semblance of your at-home fitness routine. You may have crossed a number of time zones on a red-eye flight and yet were expected to immediately perform at full throttle. If you're tired, restrain yourself from rushing back to work. You need time to recover. The idea is to work with, not against, your body's adaptive mechanism. By giving yourself a

## TRAVEL FITNESS TIPS: ARE YOU A TRAVEL JUNKIE? MAINTAINING THE WORK-FAMILY BALANCE

For some, taking to the road is more of a compulsion than a necessity. One business traveler mused, "I love to travel. I'll go any time, anywhere. I could probably travel and never come home." The adrenaline rush from traversing the globe can be an inescapable temptation. The lures of freedom, new people and places all tug at our wanderlust. Maybe after a solid month or two of being at home, a silent voice prods you: "Wouldn't it be nice to catch a plane to Europe and break up this humdrum existence? Just think, no more diaper changing, dish washing, or errands. And no one to answer to!" Let's face it, some trips have more to do with psychological payoffs than the demands of business. There's something shamelessly self-indulgent about having your bed made every morning and your meals cooked every day by someone else. Maybe you really do have to call on that distant client right away.

But wait. Like any other compulsion, travel has its rewards and its costs. By eagerly consenting to business travel—even agreeing to excursions of questionable value—the compulsive traveler may lose touch with his or her values, including the important needs of family and relationships. This can cause tension in the family circle. Pretty soon you're no longer updated on family news. You're out of the loop, a spectator in your own home. Feeling left out, you want to stay away even more. Your partner seeks comfort from others. It's a vicious circle.

There's a delicate balance between the demands of business travel and family, but one well worth finding and maintaining. "Many travelers say they don't have enough time to take care of their relationships. Then, before they know it, they don't have relationships to take care of," writes Richard J. Leider in *Training & Development.* "A little planning and extra attention may not spare you the loneliness of the road entirely; but can help you avoid the loneliness of a lifetime."

chance to regroup, you'll avoid the cycle of fatigue experienced by many harried travelers.

To recover (and ready yourself for your next trip), schedule a "lull" period and don't work at full throttle the first day or two back. Most travelers require a day or two to recover from a domestic trip and three or more for international excursions. Dr. Goldstein recommends at least a full day home, if possible, for recuperation before getting back to work. If you can't find the time, expect and plan to perform below par, he says.

The best strategy is to time your return to take advantage of a weekend recovery day. Instead of coming home the last minute on Sunday night, arrive on Friday night or Saturday morning. When you come home, do nothing for a while, advises flight attendant Linda Rocha. To readjust, she and her fellow flight attendants live by three rules: Don't make any big decisions, don't do anything major, and don't do anything dangerous. "The flight attendants always joke that we shouldn't operate any heavy equipment when we get back," she says. In fact, many of Rocha's colleagues just throw down their bags and crash.

If it's not possible to take off all the time you need (many of us can't schedule any time off after a trip), think of creative ways to ease into work. For example, schedule your work in a way that allows you to start slow and gain momentum. The first morning back, do mindless work such as preparing your expense account, sorting mail, or returning telephone calls. By the afternoon or next day, you should start to feel more oriented and motivated. As part of frequent traveler Carolyn Stahtl's recovery technique, she works out of her home for a day or two after a long trip. Working in a familiar, comfortable place helps her to find balance—and she still catches up on work.

## Returning to Fitness

Replenishing energy reserves and resuming health and fitness routines are top priorities after a trip. If you've followed the many health and fitness tips in the preceding chapters, it shouldn't be too difficult to get back in shape. But if you've slipped off the wagon during your travels—and we all indulge at one time or another—it's time to get back into your at-home fitness groove.

"After a trip, all the things that you normally think of as part of your fitness routine ought to be magnified just a little bit," says Dr. James Rippe. "You need to be a little more conscious of getting your workout in, of drinking lots of water instead of alcoholic beverages, of eating right, and relieving your stress." If you were burning the candle at both ends while away, get extra sleep. Make it a point to drink extra water to rehydrate your body after a long flight. Practice your preferred stress-reduction technique to calm your jangled nerves.

Be alert to post-trip health effects, such as jet lag and insomnia. Many travelers do their best to conquer jet lag at their destination, but don't do a thing about it when they get home. Remember: the ill effects of transmeridian travel occur at both ends of a trip. Make sure to practice the jet lag strategies outlined in Chapter 3 to get your body in sync, such as exposing yourself to bright light at appropriate times and getting some exercise. Otherwise, you'll languish with jet lag longer than you need to. The physical and emotional stress of living out of a suitcase also can trigger insomnia after a trip. Make use of Chapters 4 and 7 for strategies on achieving sound sleep and reducing stress. If you notice any unusual physical symptoms that may be travel-related, especially if you've been in Third World countries, consult immediately with a travel medicine specialist. Some diseases may not appear until after your trip.

If you've neglected your exercise regimen while away, get moving, but don't overdo it. Many returning travelers pass on exercise because they feel tired after traveling. Others fall into the "making up for lost time" trap. Ensnared in the indulge-purge syndrome, they "let go" during the trip and then work out too hard the first few weeks back. In many respects, it resembles a form of self-punishment. Their subconscious mind thinks, "I have to pay for all those lavish dinners!" These folks rush headlong into strenuous workouts, sometimes at an intensity greater than before the trip, fearing they've lost time. They're going to get thin or in shape, no matter what the cost, and too often the cost is injury.

Instead, ease back into your exercise routine. If you've neglected your workouts for a time, don't rush back and exercise at your pretrip level. Accommodate for the increased risk of injury due to travel-induced stiffness and inactivity. Your initial workouts should be shorter and less intense as you move toward your prior fitness level. For the first day or two, go slow. To gear up for your regular workouts, you might start first with a brisk walk or swim. These activities keep your body fit without undue strain. Focus also on your warm-up and cool-down. Before your workout, do four to five minutes of low-level aerobic activity, such as jogging in place, and then stretch. Avoid too much stretching before your workout because of the increased stiffness from travel. After your workout, stretch again to prevent soreness.

How long before you feel like your old self at the gym? One or two days of lighter activity will bring you up to speed and ready to resume your pretrip fitness routine, says Dr. Bagshaw.

Coming home strong is the final step in your travel fitness program. After reading this book, you have the tools to build your own travel health and fitness program. By adopting some of the healthy travel habits outlined in this book, you'll manage to keep your physical, mental, and emotional balance while on the road. Take this book along as your travel companion. Refer to it as often as you need until good travel habits become a way of life on the road.

# The Travel Health and Fitness Master Checklist

As you prepare your travel health and fitness program, it's helpful to have a checklist of "must-do" items. Below we've compiled a list of reminders to assist you in planning ahead for every aspect of travel fitness. Refer to this checklist before any trip. Revise it as needed to meet your needs. With a little practice, pretrip fitness planning will become second nature. Here's to feeling better on your next trip.

1. Identify and rank health and fitness goals.
2. Pack with fitness in mind.
3. Book flights to stay fit.
   - ❏ Given a choice, take only nonstop flights.
   - ❏ Avoid red-eye specials, hub airports, and peak travel times.
   - ❏ Schedule plenty of time for the unexpected.
   - ❏ Select an aisle, bulkhead, or exit row seat.
   - ❏ Get your boarding pass early.
   - ❏ Arrange to survive your seat by creating lumbar and neck support.
   - ❏ On international flights, request a nonsmoking seat as far away from the smoking section as possible.
   - ❏ Order a special meal.
   - ❏ Wear comfortable clothing and something warm on your feet.

❏ Bring your own water.

❏ Plan to walk the aisle, stretch, and exercise every hour or two.

❏ Pack on-board entertainment, such as music tapes or audio books.

❏ Research airline fitness perks, such as massage chairs (JAL), massages (Virgin Air), "Well-Being in the Air" (British Airways), in-flight aerobics/stretching (Lufthansa, Northwest, British Airways).

4. Select a rental or company car with features that enhance comfort.

5. Choose accommodations to increase fitness options.

❏ Call the concierge regarding access to a good health club, pool, running track, walking trail, and/or personal trainer.

❏ Ask for a bed board as needed.

6. Plan layover fitness options.

❏ Research nearby airport hotel fitness centers, access to airport "sleeping rooms" to rent.

❏ If feasible, join an airline club.

7. Design jet lag strategy.

❏ Decide whether to switch your body clock.

❏ Begin adjusting sleep before you leave.

❏ Schedule exposure to light and exercise for when you arrive.

❏ Fly east early, fly west late.

❏ Book daytime arrival.

❏ Schedule for one to two days of adjustment.

8. Plan for and schedule your workouts.

❏ Arrange business/athletic activities.

❏ Make appointment with local personal trainer.

❏ Research on- and off-site facilities/reciprocal club arrangements.

❏ Plan for in-room exercise (borrow platform or videotape from hotel; bring jump rope, water weights, and/or exercise tubing; watch early morning TV exercise show).

❏ Schedule light exercise before and after a long flight or drive.

❏ Bring along portable workout routine.

9. Plan diet strategy.

   ❏ Set diet priorities.

   ❏ Pack healthy snacks.

   ❏ Research restaurants that offer healthy, safe fare and nearby grocery stores.

10. Plan to beat stress.

   ❏ Identify your key stressors before you go.

   ❏ Make travel plans as early as possible.

   ❏ Get as much done at home and at the office as you can before leaving.

   ❏ Create in-transit contingency plans.

   ❏ Make sure your travel plans are realistic and flexible.

   ❏ Don't overschedule the first day.

   ❏ Create a reminder card of important numbers and a packing list.

   ❏ Have a plan for dealing with downtime.

   ❏ Learn about your destination.

   ❏ Plan at least one pleasurable activity.

   ❏ Arrange to meet friends, alumni, or local professional association members.

   ❏ Plan a possible weekend getaway.

   ❏ Find a way to induce the "relaxation response."

11. Arrange to sleep well and be rested.

   ❏ Get extra sleep before you go.

   ❏ Have a good at-home sleep pattern.

   ❏ Book a king-size bed.

   ❏ Bring your own pillow.

   ❏ Reserve a quiet room.

12. Consider taking family and/or partner along.

13. Obtain a detailed travel itinerary to leave with family and co-workers.

14. Schedule family time/social engagements for when you return.

15. For international travel:
    - ❏ Schedule appointment with travel medicine specialist to obtain necessary and recommended vaccinations and medications.
    - ❏ Contact international travel resources for health and cultural information.
    - ❏ Check your insurance policies and medical coverage.
16. Plan post-trip recovery period.

# References

Benson, H. (1975). *The relaxation response.* New York: Avon Books.

Brown, G. (1989). *The airline passenger's guerrilla handbook.* Washington, DC: The Blakes Publishing Group.

Cooper, R. (1989). *Health and fitness excellence.* Boston: Houghton Mifflin.

Cummings, J. (1991). *The business travel survival guide.* New York: John Wiley & Sons, Inc.

Dement, W. (1992). *The sleepwatchers.* Palo Alto, CA: Stanford Alumni Association.

Ehret, C., & Scanlon, L. (1983). *Overcoming jet lag.* New York: Berkley Books.

Gavin, J. (1992). *The exercise habit.* Champaign, IL: Leisure Press.

Gould, N. (1974). Back-pocket sciatica. *New England Journal of Medicine, 290,* 633.

Hauri, P., & Linde, S. (1991). *No more sleepless nights.* New York: John Wiley & Sons, Inc.

Jacobson, M. (1991). *Fast-food guide.* New York: Workman Publishing.

Mayes, K. (1991). *Beat jet lag.* London: Thorsons.

Tribole, E. (1992). *Eating on the run.* Champaign, IL: Leisure Press.

Zemach-Bersin, D., Zemach-Bersin, K., & Reese, M. (1990). *Relaxercise.* New York: HarperCollins.

# About the Authors

As an attorney and professional writer, **Rebecca Johnson** has done more than her fair share of business travel while pursuing story ideas and representing clients. Her writing has appeared in many publications, including *People* magazine, *San Francisco Business*, *The Tucson Citizen*, and *The Legal Marketing Report*.

Rebecca earned her JD in 1984 from the University of San Diego School of Law. She is a member of the Authors' Guild and Women in Communications, Inc. She is also a fitness enthusiast who enjoys running, mountain biking, horseback riding, hiking, and tennis.

**Bill Tulin** is a San Francisco-based attorney and business executive who travels extensively on business—often more than 100,000 flight miles per year. He is also a National Strength and Conditioning Association Certified Strength and Conditioning Specialist (CSCS), a personal trainer, and former physical education instructor at San Diego State University. Combining his travel, conditioning, and business expertise, he counsels other travelers facing the challenges of maintaining their workout regimens on the road.

In 1985 Bill earned his JD and in 1988 he earned an advanced law degree (LL.M.) in business taxation at John Marshall School of Law in Chicago. He is a member of the U.S. Masters Swimming Association and Freestyle Players' Association. Bill trains almost daily in a variety of athletic disciplines.

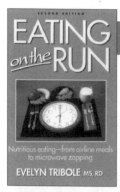
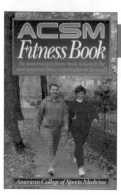